NURTURING
BOYS
TO BE
BETTER
MEN

Gender Equality Starts at Home

Shelly Vaziri Flais, MD, FAAP

American Academy of Pediatrics
DEDICATED TO THE HEALTH OF ALL CHILDREN®

American Academy of Pediatrics Publishing Staff

Mary Lou White, *Chief Product and Services Officer/SVP, Membership, Marketing, and Publishing*

Mark Grimes, *Vice President, Publishing*

Holly Kaminski, *Editor, Consumer Publishing*

Caroline Heller, PhD, *Digital Content Editor*

Shannan Martin, *Production Manager, Consumer Publications*

Amanda Helmholz, *Medical Copy Editor*

Sara Hoerdeman, *Marketing and Acquisitions Manager, Consumer Products*

Published by the American Academy of Pediatrics

345 Park Blvd

Itasca, IL 60143

Telephone: 630/626-6000

Facsimile: 847/434-8000

www.aap.org

The American Academy of Pediatrics is an organization of 67,000 primary care pediatricians, pediatric medical subspecialists, and pediatric surgical specialists dedicated to the health, safety, and well-being of all infants, children, adolescents, and young adults.

The information contained in this publication should not be used as a substitute for the medical care and advice of your pediatrician. There may be variations in treatment that your pediatrician may recommend based on individual facts and circumstances.

Statements and opinions expressed are those of the author and not necessarily those of the American Academy of Pediatrics.

Any websites, brand names, products, or manufacturers are mentioned for informational and identification purposes only and do not imply an endorsement by the American Academy of Pediatrics (AAP). The AAP is not responsible for the content of external resources. Information was current at the time of publication.

The publishers have made every effort to trace the copyright holders for borrowed materials. If they have inadvertently overlooked any, they will be pleased to make the necessary arrangements at the first opportunity.

This publication has been developed by the American Academy of Pediatrics. The contributors are expert authorities in the field of pediatrics. No commercial involvement of any kind has been solicited or accepted in the development of the content of this publication. Disclosures: The author reports no disclosures.

Every effort is made to keep *Nurturing Boys to Be Better Men: Gender Equality Starts at Home* consistent with the most recent advice and information available from the American Academy of Pediatrics.

Special discounts are available for bulk purchases of this publication. Email Special Sales at nationalaccounts@aap.org for more information.

Printed in the United States of America

9-503   1 2 3 4 5 6 7 8 9 10

CB0134

ISBN: 978-1-61002-677-2

eBook: 978-1-61002-679-6

EPUB: 978-1-61002-678-9

Cover and publication design by Scott Rattray Design

Library of Congress Control Number: 2022921657

ALSO AVAILABLE FROM THE AMERICAN ACADEMY OF PEDIATRICS

By Shelly Vaziri Flais, MD, FAAP

Raising Twins: Parenting Multiples From Pregnancy Through the School Years

Caring for Your School-Age Child: Ages 5–12

Additional Books for Families

Baby and Toddler Basics: Expert Answers to Parents' Top 150 Questions

Building Happier Kids: Stress-busting Tools for Parents

Building Resilience in Children and Teens: Giving Kids Roots and Wings

Caring for Your Baby and Young Child: Birth to Age 5*

Co-parenting Through Separation and Divorce: Putting Your Children First

Congrats—You're Having a Teen! Strengthen Your Family and Raise a Good Person

Heading Home With Your Newborn: From Birth to Reality

High Five Discipline: Positive Parenting for Happy, Healthy, Well-Behaved Kids

My Child Is Sick! Expert Advice for Managing Common Illnesses and Injuries

The New Baby Blueprint: Caring for You and Your Little One

Raising an Organized Child: 5 Steps to Boost Independence, Ease Frustration, and Promote Confidence

Retro Baby: Timeless Activities to Boost Development—Without All the Gear!

Retro Toddler: More Than 100 Old-School Activities to Boost Development

Return to You: A Postpartum Plan for New Moms

Quirky Kids: Understanding and Supporting Your Child With Developmental Differences

The Working Mom Blueprint: Winning at Parenting Without Losing Yourself

You-ology: A Puberty Guide for Every Body

*This book is also available in Spanish.

Pluripotent
From Oxford Languages
plu • ri • po • tent
/ˌplo͞orəˈpōtnt/
adjective
BIOLOGY
(of an immature or stem cell)
capable of giving rise to several different
cell types

To all children, filled with potential, who give rise to
a constantly evolving and improving future, and to my
own sons and daughter, who have been my best teachers

PLEASE NOTE

The author respects and acknowledges the diversity and range of the gender spectrum and gender identity. Please note that for the entirety of this book, when we refer to to *girls* and *women,* we are referencing those who identify as female. When we refer to *boys* and *men,* we are referencing those who identify as male. We recognize those individuals who have a gender other than their sex assignment at birth and those for whom their gender is fluid.

WHAT PEOPLE ARE SAYING ABOUT
NURTURING BOYS TO BE BETTER MEN

Parents who are thinking critically about gender roles and equality will find an abundance of guidance, conversation starters, and practical tips that are actually implementable! This book can help the next generation of boys find freedom to own and un-define their masculinity and learn to become safe spaces for themselves.

Justin Baldoni, author of *Man Enough* and *Boys Will Be Human*

A must-read for any parent looking to develop young men who are the future to creating meaningful change in our homes and workplaces.

David G. Smith, PhD, associate professor in the Johns Hopkins Carey Business School and coauthor of *Good Guys: How Men Can Be Allies for Women in the Workplace*

In her deeply practical book, Dr Flais makes the compelling point that raising a son able to relate to the new world of gender equity is better than helping him unlearn habits ill-suited to the times he lives in. With the eye of a pediatrician and the care of a mother, she suggests concrete ways parents can help their son, at each stage of his life, consider what equity actually means. In so doing, she takes a strong stand against biases that hold low expectations for boys and models the kind of accountability that will bring that new world closer.

Michael Reichert, PhD, author of *How to Raise a Boy: The Power of Connection to Build Good Men* and director of the Center for the Study of Boys' and Girls' Lives at the University of Pennsylvania

So many people want to raise their boys differently—but don't know how. It is the "how" that is hard. That is why *Nurturing Boys to Be Better Men: Gender Equality Begins at Home* will be such a welcomed help to so many parents. Dr Vaziri Flais' practical, real-life examples are easy for all of us to try at home. The life-cycle approach is helpful, offering advice to those parenting boys of all ages. And I love the way Dr Vaziri Flais brings in the importance of the community. Sure, we parents have a lot of influence. But anyone with a boy in their life—grandparents, friends, neighbors, teachers—everyone has something to learn and something to contribute.

Kate Mangino, PhD, author of *Equal Partners: Improving Gender Equality at Home*

This is a topic that is often not actively addressed yet is so impactful. Dr Flais provides more than just background as to why it's important to promote gender equality. Throughout her book, she offers a template to start conversations with boys of all ages and, more importantly, how to make these discussions a normal part of everyday life.

> David Stukus, MD, clinical professor of pediatrics, author of *Allergies and Adolescents: Transitioning Towards Independent Living*, and husband and father of 2 children

Dr Flais offers a thoughtful, compassionately written book. She highlights the needs of families in 2023, to create meaningful, doable family lives with participation from partners and children of all genders. Parents will find realistic expectations for small steps toward having the daily routines they want!

> Alanna Higgins Joyce, MD, MPH, associate professor, Northwestern University Feinberg School of Medicine, and mom of 3 boys

As a pediatrician and mom of 3 boys, I believe Dr Vaziri Flais' words provide a helpful road map for parents as they guide their sons through life. As a parent, I want my boys to be kind and compassionate and to realize their dreams and to not have those dreams be limited by what the world may say those dreams should look like. This book helps start the conversation for families as they work to provide a supportive environment in which to raise their children and help them be all they can be.

> Nicole DuPraw Carter, MD, FAAP, pediatrician, Auburn, AL, and mother of 3 boys

As a collective society, we bemoan the inequality between men and women but do little to rectify the societal norms that impede change. Dr Flais has created a road map for parents to change our preconceived notions of raising both boys and girls. This book is an important step toward reaching gender equality both at home and in the workplace and should be on the "must-read" list for every expectant parent.

> Sarah Lacey, MD, FAAP, community pediatrician, Denver, CO

EQUITY, DIVERSITY, AND INCLUSION STATEMENT

The American Academy of Pediatrics is committed to principles of equity, diversity, and inclusion in its publishing program. Editorial boards, author selections, and author transitions (publication succession plans) are designed to include diverse voices that reflect society as a whole. Editor and author teams are encouraged to actively seek out diverse authors and reviewers at all stages of the editorial process. Publishing staff are committed to promoting equity, diversity, and inclusion in all aspects of publication writing, review, and production.

Contents

xi

It is easier to build strong children than to repair broken men.

FREDERICK DOUGLASS

Introduction

Changing the World With Intention Within Our Homes

When my youngest child was born, my twin sons were 2 years old and my oldest son was 3½ years old. In the haze of keeping 4 kids younger than 4 years old fed and alive, I'm not sure I would be able to remember what remains as one of the most favorite moments I've experienced as a parent without the assistance of modern technology. Thanks to digital photos, I have proof that reminds me that this particular moment did indeed occur. My newborn, the new kid on the block, as it were, was carefully swaddled, peacefully napping in a bassinet strategically positioned by a sunny kitchen window amid the chaos of our home: two 2-year-old boys and one 3-year-old boy going about their toddler business. Surely, this newborn must have felt quite comfortable with listening to the sounds and environment she had gestated within over the prior 9 months, for she slept wonderfully.

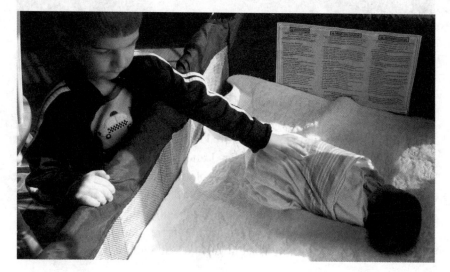

My 3-year-old son interrupted his play to instinctively place a protective hand onto the baby, at a distance away from her face as his parents had repeatedly instructed, to check on her well-being. Moments later—perhaps mimicking his older brother, perhaps channeling the responsible, loving traits he would exhibit for years to come—one of my 2-year-old twin sons placed a gentle hand onto my newborn's swaddled knees, checking on her (yes, still sleeping soundly) status. I praised the action, and my son, for his nurturing instincts. The photographic images of this day, so many years ago, are priceless to me as a mom, the memories being even more so, and illustrate how inherently loving young children are, even as toddlers. Kids are born with a limitless capacity to love and care for others.

All young children have inborn personality traits and temperaments, as well as a large capacity to love, empathize with, and nurture others. As a parent in that moment in the sunny kitchen, I did not shoo my young sons away from my newborn. Rather, I encouraged them, complimented them for being gentle with the baby, explained how the baby's breathing was normal, and described aloud with words what we were observing. Yes, life with a newborn is a blur, yet I consciously worked to send my sons daily messages that they were part of our new baby's posse and that their consideration was noted, acknowledged, and appreciated. Instead of emphasizing what my toddler sons *shouldn't* do, I informed them, through positive reinforcement, what they *could* do, and I encouraged them to continue to follow their loving instincts.

At the time of this writing, my 3 sons are now in college, and my youngest, no longer a swaddled infant, is on her final stretch of high school. For over 2 decades, I've had the privilege of a front row seat witnessing these babies become capable young adults. Like all families do, we've had our share of challenges, including childhood cancer and divorce, giving us plenty of real-world situations in which to support each other and practice empathy and resilience. My personal parenting experience and my professional clinical practice in pediatrics have been intertwined all these years, with each road heavily influencing the other. Neither experience has occurred in a vacuum. As a physician caring for infants and children through young adulthood, I've witnessed a diverse array of family structures, backgrounds, and situations play out over the course of years. Serving as a medical home for families means I ride a years-long journey with my patients' families. As a clinician in a typical bustling workday, I'll go from one exam room in which I've discussed a toddler's developmental progress with a parent to another exam room in which a teen is dealing with mental health struggles. I'm privileged to serve our patients' families and it has given me perspective to take the long view on child development. To raise an infant through young adulthood, to wrestle through the day-to-day chaos to support larger, big-picture goals, is a humbling experience. It is living these 2 intertwined roads, both professional and personal, that informs my perspective and approach within the pages of this book.

SPEAKING OUR GOALS INTO EXISTENCE

I remember an out-of-state family gathering one summer when my sons were all toddlers and preschoolers; extended relatives, watching the cousin chaos, knowingly nodding, repeating the phrase "boys will be boys" as I shuddered inside. I am not a fan of that phrase, from both a kid perspective and an adult perspective. There's a sort of self-fulfilling prophecy that happens when kids hear such phrases spoken within earshot. From the adult perspective, certain behaviors could be left unchecked by the surrounding caregivers with an assumption that "boys will be boys."

All too often, we hear of 2- and 3-year-old kids, especially boys, whom others have branded as "difficult toddlers," "terrible twos," or "threenagers," a term doubly frustrating for me as a pediatrician and a mom, as it essentially throws a whole other age-group under the bus with an insulting, usually inaccurate generalization. These tiresome clichés often result from momentary outbursts when the young child is, in fact, behaving developmentally appropriately and acting out. These outbursts are more frequent if the child is overtired, due to eat, or a combination of the two, otherwise known as "hangry." Separate from these outbursts, if you stop to observe a toddler over the course of a day, you will discover many moments of nurturing, whether it's steadfastly clinging to their "lovey" or another comfort object (eg, a beloved blanket) or, in my family's case, ensuring the comfort and safety of their newborn sister. Is it surprising that these loving moments are observed in toddler *boys*? I'd like to think not.

EVOLVING MESSAGING

How often does our society send our young sons other, different messages? How often do parents, teachers, family, friends, and the media simply assume that young boys will be wild, uncontrollable, and overly physical? And in turn, how much of these messages are internalized by our boys and perpetuated through the generations?

Younger boys, as early as toddlers, absorb messaging from the world around us about what kind of toys they should play with, or activities they can engage in, or which skills or personality traits they may have. Toy trains, or dolls? Mimicking caregiving tasks such as cooking, or rambunctious play? Assertive, or a good listener? By fourth and fifth grades, many kids have already assigned particular attributes (eg, "emotional," "aggressive") to people with a particular gender. To quote Chimamanda Ngozi Adichie in her 2012 book *We Should All Be Feminists*, "The problem with gender is that it prescribes how we *should* be rather than recognizing how we are." Rather than having to unlearn lessons of gender that were internalized while growing up, our sons, supported by a proactive awareness and approach, can become who they are meant to be, free of gender-based stereotypes.

Parents should have conversations with each other to discuss what kind of messaging they want for their son. Do words such as *caring, sensitive, wise, good friend, kind, honest*, and *smart* come to mind? Even as early as pregnancy, parents and their partners can begin a conversation about goals for their son and create a road map to nurture their son as a whole, complete individual.

I've thought long and hard about the issue of gender expectations, not only from the perspective of a female physician working in a historically male profession but also as the mom of 3 beautiful sons. I vividly remember an ultrasound midway through my twin pregnancy that revealed I was carrying 2 boys, who would join my then 1-year-old older son. At that moment, even when two-thirds of my sons were still in utero, I began to consider: if I were to be surrounded by—and, more importantly, raising—3 young men, knowing what I know about male stereotypes and toxic masculinity, what steps could I take as a parent to defy these prevalent generational and societal messages? How could I help my sons not only become full humans in touch with their creative, nurturing sides, as much as their athletic, physical sides, but also become empathic, educated allies?

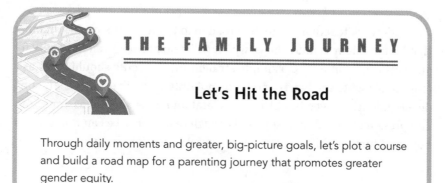

THE FAMILY JOURNEY

Let's Hit the Road

Through daily moments and greater, big-picture goals, let's plot a course and build a road map for a parenting journey that promotes greater gender equity.

CREATE YOUR OWN JOURNEY

Each child begins life with certain inborn characteristics and personality traits; however, they can still be considered a fresh, blank slate that has yet to absorb the messaging from families, society, and prior generations. We all have the power to influence this messaging. Much progress has been made, but there is more to do. You and your partner will want to have ongoing conversations, starting in pregnancy, about how your home life will look and how the tasks of raising kids and maintaining a household should be shared, divided, and modeled for your son. What *messaging* do you, as parents, wish to share with your son as he grows through infancy into young adulthood? What *role modeling* can you do as a parent to encourage the pattern?

My book will seek the following **3 main goals** to promote greater generational gender equality:

1. Promote a whole-child approach, recognizing our sons as capable of the full range of human emotions despite generational perpetuation of the idea of "male" characteristics.
2. Use an ages-and-stages developmental approach, recognizing opportunities for growth and awareness not only within the child-parent relationship but also in how our sons interact with extended family, school, and the greater outside community.
3. Propose how parents can best model gender equity for our sons, for as the expression goes, "kids do as they see."

Let's work together to create a road map to raise our sons in a manner that honors them as individuals, which will help promote gender equity for all. This road will not be a simple straight line. Parents should work as a team to navigate the twists and turns not only through each of their son's developmental stages but also as societal and generational assumptions and pressures reveal themselves. Through teamwork, we can nurture our boys and further shift society toward greater gender equity.

Chapter 1

Nurturing Boys to Be Better Men: How Can We Promote Gender Equity in Our Homes?

As a female born in the '70s and raised in the '70s and '80s, I was told by my family, teachers, and the world around me, "You can do and be whatever you want to be." I wanted to be a doctor from a very early age; for me, it was a no-brainer because I not only gravitated to science and math but also loved the social aspect of communicating with and helping others. I never, at any moment, wondered how I would juggle a physician's demanding career with raising a family and children. Completely naively, I figured that society would have figured everything out by the time I became an adult. Surely, our world would have sorted out the logistics of gendered parenting by the time it was my turn to have my own kids, as a practicing physician? Sadly, my experiences along the way revealed that this was not the case.

Growing up in the '70s and '80s, were the boys my age hearing messaging from parents, families, schools, and society that *they* could "be whatever they want to be"? Oh yes, of course. Was anyone telling the boys of the '70s and '80s that they should step up and be equal parents and partners sharing in the tasks of running a household as they get older, including supporting their brilliant partners on their own respective paths? Unfortunately, I don't think so, but we can, and must, change this inequity. Raising my own sons in the 21st century, reflecting on what I've experienced and observed professionally and personally over the past few decades, I've been very conscious of the messaging I want to give my own children. I feel we can, and should, do better.

More than merely being told they have an equal share in household work, and being trained in how to do this over the years and age-appropriate stages, boys need messaging that they're allowed to be whole, complete humans. All too often, they're put into a small box of competition, sports, and power, with the corresponding machismo characteristics. To this point, in a 2021 NPR interview, former President Barack Obama reflected, "We're very comfortable, I think, . . . in saying to girls 'You can do anything you want. . . . You can be girly, you can be a tomboy, you can be ambitious, you can be more reserved. . .' With boys, we still say 'sports, money, physical strength, girls.' . . . It's which chimp has the most bananas."[1]

GENDER EQUITY VERSUS GENDER EQUALITY

Let us take a moment to define some terms, specifically gender *equity* and gender *equality.* During the early stages of the production of this book, the Publishing team discussed which word, what goal, we were striving for. According to the George Washington University Milken Institute School of Public Health, "*Equality* means each individual or group of people is given the same resources or opportunities. *Equity* recognizes that each person has different circumstances and allocates the exact resources and opportunities needed to reach an equal outcome."[2] Recognizing the inherent differences among the genders, sexes, and, frankly, all of us as people, as well as understanding generational imbalances that have come before us, *equity,* as equal of a playing field as possible, is what we are striving for.

LET'S START A CONVERSATION

This book aspires to start conversations between parents. A single conversation alone, however, is not enough. This book aims to create templates for ongoing conversations: with our partners, with our sons as they grow, with our families and friends, with our coworkers and bosses, and, perhaps most importantly, with ourselves. We may have great intentions; however,

1. Shahani A. *Art of Power.* Barack Obama redefines what it means to be a man. May 13, 2021. Accessed May 16, 2023. https://www.wbez.org/stories/barack-obama-redefines-what-it-means -to-be-a-man/9cb514f8-7d89-43da-8912-b34399789771.

2. MPH@GW, the George Washington University online Master of Public Health program. Equity vs. equality: what's the difference? November 5, 2020. Accessed May 16, 2023. https://onlinepublichealth. gwu.edu/resources/equity-vs-equality.

there will be moments when we realize we could have, or can, do better. There will also be situations when societal and generational pressures reveal themselves, thwarting our efforts, as well-intentioned as they may be. I, personally, have certainly experienced this pressure throughout my parenthood experience thus far. At the time of this writing, I have 3 young adults in college and 1 adolescent in high school, yet I still have so much to learn! I have the humility to realize I am far from perfect myself and far from "done." A *growth mindset,* coupled with humility, is the key ingredient for these ongoing conversations to promote gender equality.

As both a parent and a child health expert, I believe we can raise our sons in a manner that promotes a more gender-equitable world. A beautiful privilege of caring for my patients' families for years, often following the growth of a child from the newborn stage through high school and beyond, is following along the family's journey, sharing notes, and learning from each other as time passes. One goal of this book is for it to serve as a practical, daily how-to manual to raise boys with the theme and goal of greater gender equality. We pediatricians consider a child's development in an ages-and-stages manner; accordingly, this book will help parents recognize opportunities as early as pregnancy through infancy, toddler stages, preschool years, grade school, middle school, and high school to promote a whole-child approach, a gender-equity framework, that ultimately benefits *all* children through male growth and allyship.

Just as daily toothbrushing helps promote lifelong dental health, everyday decisions and interactions can influence societal shifts. Girls have gotten a message about gender equity for decades, and now this book will help parents flip the script and focus on our *sons,* who, among many other benefits, deserve the opportunity to serve as equal partners and full parents, not just "babysitters," to their future children, should they choose to become parents. Some define feminism as treating women as full humans, and along this theme, this book examines how we can raise our sons with a whole-child approach, recognizing *boys'* full range of temperament and personalities, preventing perpetuated toxic masculinity. Peggy Orenstein, in her article "The Miseducation of the American Boy," noted, "Feminism may have provided girls with a powerful alternative to conventional femininity, and a language with which to express the myriad problems-that-have-no-name, but there have been no credible equivalents for boys." So, together, let's broaden and expand what it means to be male.

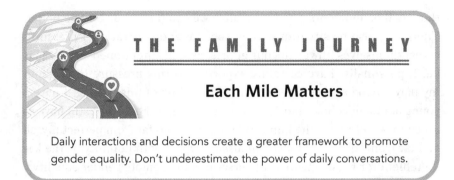

THE FAMILY JOURNEY

Each Mile Matters

Daily interactions and decisions create a greater framework to promote gender equality. Don't underestimate the power of daily conversations.

PROMOTE GREATER GENERATIONAL GENDER EQUITY

A theme of parenthood in general, and in this book specifically, is that day-to-day decisions and interactions add up to create a framework that can influence society in a positive way and move the needle toward greater gender equality. Let's dive into our 3 main goals to explore further how our daily actions will cause a generational ripple of change.

Goal 1. Promote a whole-child approach, recognizing our sons as capable of the full range of human emotions despite generational perpetuation of the idea of "male" characteristics.

Each chapter of this book has a specific section that discusses a child's evolving temperament and personality and how that evolution plays into a greater framework of gender equity. We as parents should "allow" a boy to be a whole child with the full range of emotions and character traits, including empathy and caregiving. Pediatricians love the expression "meet the child where they are."

At face value, most of us would agree that as individual humans, we have a wide range of personality traits and characteristics. Yet all too often as a society, we tend to assign labels, stereotypes, and preconceived notions to one's sex assignment at birth. How often do we hear that women are natural multitaskers and caregivers? As it turns out, men can also be empathic, nurturing multitaskers; labeling them otherwise can lead to toxic masculinity that harms society as a whole. Each time I post a photo to social media of my teenaged son cooking, the shocked comments flabbergasted that my sons are capable cooks and bakers remind me we have a long way to go. Everyday routines, role modeling, and daily decisions and interactions will help create a greater, broader worldview for our sons. To quote Peggy Orenstein, in her article, "The Miseducation of the American Boy," from *The Atlantic,* "[I]t's time to rethink assumptions about how we raise boys. That will require models of manhood that are neither ashamed nor regressive, and that emphasize emotional flexibility—a hallmark of mental health. Stoicism is valuable sometimes, as is free expression; toughness and tenderness can coexist in one human."

Shelly Vaziri Flais
Mar 7, 2014 · 👥

Apple turnover success!

We will examine these issues in the manner that pediatricians assess a child's development: by ages and stages. When our children are *infants or toddlers,* how do we navigate gender stereotypes and identity? When our boys reach *middle and high school,* how do our sons themselves navigate gender stereotypes and identity? Each chapter suggests consuming media (eg, books, television shows, films, online videos, social media, video games) *together* to identify teachable moments, including surprising or inappropriate situations, and to ask open-ended questions to spur discussions (eg, "What did you think of that?" or "How would you have handled that situation?").

THE FAMILY JOURNEY

The Silver Lining of a Wrong Turn

There will be gaffes and missteps along the way. Reframe these as teachable moments, for your son and for yourself.

Goal 2. Use an ages-and-stages developmental approach, recognizing opportunities for growth and awareness not only within the child-parent relationship but also in how our sons interact with extended family, school, and the greater outside community.

This book serves as a how-to guide to coach parents and walk through and role-play scenarios and interactions with family, grandparents, neighbors, and our larger communities. None of us exist in a bubble, and our views and awareness are shaped not only within our families and homes but by our interactions with the outside world. As our sons grow, consuming media together (eg, television shows, films, video games) that depicts or perpetuates certain gender roles and stereotypes can be a teachable moment, ripe for discussion to exchange ideas and share values. We parents would be wise to adopt an attitude of curiosity and learning as our kids grow into tweens and teens. Some situations, especially when speaking up to others in our community, may feel uncomfortable, but often, we will be thanked by others and will be told "Oh, I didn't think of that!" Each of us as parents has the power to plant a seed and cause a ripple effect within our friend groups, families, and communities. Just as a thin stream of water can etch out a canyon over time, daily interactions and everyday scenarios can shape a whole child's ethos and change a generation.

We will discuss how parents can start conversations: with our partners, with our sons, with loved ones, and with ourselves. As is my nature, I will provide a positive tone; rather than "don't this, don't that," we will strive toward a "try this, try that" approach, with a curious, empathetic tone. As parents, we will all stumble from time to time; this is not only OK but expected as we move forward on our journey of lifelong learning and improvement. We all have room to grow. We as parents might not even realize how certain daily or routine choices perpetuate the patriarchy within our families or communities; it can be difficult to even identify learning opportunities because some of these traditions and systems have been in place for generations. This book empathically illustrates and *anticipates* scenarios to help normalize gender-equitable behaviors. Parents can be proactive and ready for the moment. Have you ever looked back on an interaction (eg, if a grandparent steered your 4-year-old son toward the toy trucks and away from the play kitchen) and thought to yourself "Oh, I should have said XYZ instead." Plenty of well-intentioned people will do or say things that do not promote gender equity—even ourselves! We will examine these situations to recognize how we can do, and lead, better.

Goal 3. Propose how parents can best model gender equity for our sons, for as the expression goes, "kids do as they see."

The patriarchy results from generations of societal and cultural patterns; we've made much progress in the past century, but there is still much to be done. My personal perspective is as a daughter of an immigrant from the Middle East. Iran is a country well-known for limiting women's options for life, family, and careers. As a baby of the '70s, I was incredibly fortunate that despite this cultural background, I was never treated differently than my 2 older brothers. I declared in kindergarten that I would one day become a doctor, and my parents cheered me on the entire time. I am aware of my privilege and of my extreme luck to have had this encouragement literally all my life.

Along these lines, because girls have gotten the message for decades that "you are strong, you can be whatever you dream," society and our institutions still need to catch up to this "new" reality. We as a society, and as families and parents, need to speak with our *boys* on these issues. These conversations will differ at each child's developmental stages, and perhaps even more important than mere discussion, "walking the walk" and *modeling* for our children what gender roles can look like will promote gender equity.

As a practical, daily how-to manual, this book will help parents feel empowered to enact change. From a practical standpoint, when we consider what happens in our larger society, by watching the news, becoming aware of patriarchy-supporting systems, or scrolling online, it is easy to feel powerless to enact change. We as individual parents may not have the ability to mandate a national parental leave policy, for example, but we *do* have the power to raise our sons in a proactive, positive manner that will shape their views of women, men, gender roles, and how people relate and interact. Arthur Ashe has famously said, "Start where you are. Use what you have. Do what you can."

THE FAMILY JOURNEY

Choose Your Route

You have more power than you realize to enact societal change. You're raising a tiny human, from infancy into future adulthood. How you nurture your son and the experiences you share will have a ripple effect on your community and on society as a whole for years to come.

WHAT WE NEED TO DO

We are all here on this planet today because of a pregnancy, yet even in the 21st century, many of our institutions and corporations still seem surprised that over half our world population gives birth and breastfeeds. Our greater institutions, especially in the United States, have yet to normalize parental leave, and there is much work to be done to create a greater culture of robust parent support and policies. Equitable paternal leave is a huge opportunity to establish cohesive, balanced parenting roles and a healthy division of parental labor (we will discuss the topic of parental leave further in Chapters 2, Nurturing Our Sons to Be Better Men, Even Before They Are Born, and 3, Nurturing Infants to Be Better Men). Childbirth and infant care are basic functions of human life that should be normalized for all.

This book is *timely:* the global pandemic that dominated 2020, the COVID-19 pandemic, has disproportionately affected women. It has revealed and exacerbated existing cracks in our system that have pushed many women away from paid work and back toward the unpaid labor of caregiving: helping children navigate remote school, filling in child care gaps, and caring for older relatives. As I've watched this inequity unfold during the pandemic, I've continued conversations with all my children about the roles we play in society and about the multiple solutions to these societal problems we can apply to help women and men alike. What can we do today to support our sons if they choose to become parents later in their lives? It's easy to feel powerless, but there are actionable steps we can take to stem the tide of generations of patriarchy. We *do* have power; we can raise our sons by keeping the paraphrased words of Mother Teresa in mind: "If you want to change the world, go home and love your family."

We *are* making generational progress. Despite the trauma brought on by the global COVID-19 pandemic, there has been a silver lining of fathers and non-birthing parents taking on greater parenting and household roles. Studies confirm that the pandemic has resulted in more fathers taking on increased caregiving roles and housework. If a father isn't commuting to an office, he has more time with which to prepare the family meal. The household workload has been eye opening for partners who are now making school lunches, ensuring backpacks are filled with homework, and assisting kids with school necessities. We shouldn't have to rely on a global pandemic to shake up the manner in which our families operate. There is still much to be done.

Readers, a practical note: Obviously, you'll pay closer attention to the chapter corresponding to your son's current age. Additionally, I strongly suggest you read ahead to the *next* age (ie, chapter), as this will empower you to proactively *anticipate* and be ready for the next parenting stage. The great irony of parenthood is that it is *ever-changing:* as soon as we've "figured out" our kids' current stage, they've already grown and advanced to the next stage. Reading ahead a chapter at a time will help you stay ahead of the game and keep your parenting goals in focus and at the front of your mind. Thank you for engaging in this ongoing, important conversation with me.

NO ONE-SIZE-FITS-ALL SOLUTION

All too often, parenting books are met with a degree of suspicion: What do those so-called experts know anyway? In my life as a primary care pediatrician in clinical practice, I work daily to share evidence-based information and recommendations with the families I care for. As a parenting book author, I scroll social media online and cringe at posts that give parenting books a bad rap. As a parent of 4 myself, I know firsthand that each child is an individual and each family is unique. No particular scenario can be discussed and solved through absolutes. Each child is unique, and no one knows a child better than their own parent. Every family is distinctive in its makeup and day-to-day operations. The best parenting books and advice recognize the *broad spectrum* of humanity, and they acknowledge the reality that there are no one-size-fits-all solutions for the issues we face.

I've been fortunate to author books about raising twins, caring for a school-aged child, and more, and each experience has been extremely humbling. Some child health and parenting advice is pretty straightforward. For example, cigarette smoking around an infant or a young child can increase that child's chance of developing respiratory complications and ear infections. A lot of parenting deals with the fuzzy stuff, however. Will time-outs work for your toddler? What are the best ways to encourage a 5-year-old with picky eating? Many parenting conundrums are one-size-fits-all scenarios.

And that's just it, isn't it? Parenthood itself is *humbling*. Any parent of a 1-month-old infant whose poop has just exploded out of their diaper and up their back, soiling themselves and anyone within a 5-foot radius, has had a reality check. There are no easy answers to the issues faced in parenthood.

LET'S CONTINUE THE CONVERSATION

This book is not an expert perched standing at a lectern telling you what *to* do and what *not* to do. This book is a *conversation*. An important conversation. An ongoing conversation. This book stems from my utter shock and disbelief as the mom of 3 young men in the 21st century that there are still societal patterns in place that perpetuate the generational cycle of the patriarchy. My big question continues: How can we, as parents,

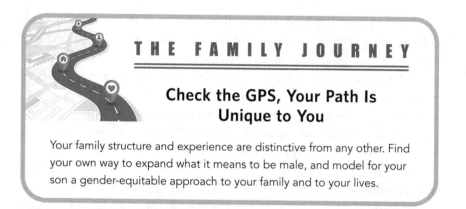

THE FAMILY JOURNEY

Check the GPS, Your Path Is Unique to You

Your family structure and experience are distinctive from any other. Find your own way to expand what it means to be male, and model for your son a gender-equitable approach to your family and to your lives.

stem this tide? Let's work together to create a family road map to promote gender equity.

Author and activist Ibram X. Kendi, of the outstanding book *How to Be an Antiracist,* tells us that to combat racism, it's not enough to not be racist; we must actively work to be anti-racist. Similarly, it's not enough to be pro gender equity; we must actively work to create better men who are allies to women in order to balance decades of generational inequities. This work occurs in daily run-of-the-mill moments, as well as broader decisions you'll make for your son as time and the years pass.

I have 3 sons who are in college at the time of this writing. I've attended family gatherings and heard relatives say "Oh well, boys will be boys." I've watched in my clinic as parents eagerly attend a newborn's initial pediatric checkups together, followed by a paternity leave ending, and then, consequently, I mostly see a mom for visits as time goes on. I also have many patients for whom their father is the usual parent to bring the child in.

Since I am not speaking at a lectern—rather, I am humbly engaging in a conversation with a growth mindset—I wanted this book to be the voice of many. In this spirit, I spoke with other families and colleagues and drew from the growing list of resources on the subject. I wanted this book to reflect the *diversity* of experiences with raising sons in the modern era. I wanted to hear not only about people's successes but also about the times during which they stumbled. I have certainly stumbled along the path, leaving an interaction or a conversation and realizing I could have done better, and I share those stories here so you can do better. Being proactive and mindful, we can enact progress.

This is a proactive book to help all of us be ready for the moments and daily decisions that carry significant impact. You may agree with some of my points and disagree with other suggestions, and this is OK. My goal is not for readers to nod in agreement from cover to cover. My goal is to make you think and to spark conversations between you, your partner, your family, your communities, and, most importantly, your son as he grows. Take your unique experiences and perspective on these issues and your ideas to your son and the world around him.

Parenting is a wild road. It's true that our generations have thought much harder about the act of parenting itself than previous generations. It's a combination of the small, everyday decisions coupled with our big-picture goals. Let's tackle both. Silence reinforces the status quo. Meaningful change occurs with thought, intention, and conversation.

Feminism means to allow women to be fully human, with a spectrum of possibilities available to them. Just as importantly, men are also fully human and should have options. One mom I spoke with (a parent of 1 girl and 2 boys) wants "equity for men" in that they can also be caring, nurturing, expressive of their emotions, and empathic. A wise dad I spoke with said he wants to "raise my sons to not be jerks." I thought about making that sentiment the title of the book but will, at a minimum, channel the spirit of it throughout these pages. Again, thank you for engaging in this ongoing, important conversation with me.

Chapter 2

Nurturing Our Sons to Be Better Men, Even Before They Are Born

How often do you see an incisively hilarious comedian perform a lengthy stand-up routine while visibly pregnant? Historically, the field of comedians has been dominated by men, yet the inimitable Ali Wong has performed a filmed comedy special while quite far along in her pregnancy not once but twice (one taped special per pregnancy)! A woman performing her occupation while far along in pregnancy should neither be surprising nor seem abnormal to anyone living in the 21st century, yet here we are. In one special, Wong asks, "A lot of people like to ask me 'Ali, how on earth do you balance family and career?' Men never get asked that question, because they don't." She's spot on with this observation.

FAMILY LIFE EXPERIENCES

I'm all in favor of every visible (literally visible, in this case) effort in society to *normalize* the state of pregnancy in particular and, in general, the full breadth of female experiences. For too long, pregnancy has been deemed something to hide. Even though the 1950s sitcom *I Love Lucy* was named for its star, Lucille Ball, her real-life pregnancy was hidden to viewers, with countless examples since. Wong fills a much-needed space to document and laugh at life from a female perspective. Any of us who have experienced the physical feats and emotional roller coaster of pregnancy and parenthood already know that human procreation is a rich source of comedic material. Practically speaking, mining the endless humor in childbirth is not just great content but a smart business move, tapping into a historically untapped market eager for more stories told about female life experiences.

Pregnancy Highlights Inequity

Creating a new life is a big, big deal. Anyone who has experienced pregnancy, in addition to deserving a huge trophy, has the inevitable moments of wonder that the human species has survived for as long as it has. Pregnancy is supposed to be "natural," but frankly, many aspects of pregnancy do not *feel* natural at all. The state of being pregnant, while a wonderful blessing, is, frankly speaking, somewhat surreal and science fiction–y. For the duration of each of my pregnancies, I was elated at the prospect of meeting each new child, but honestly, I was reminded of the 1979 iconic science fiction film by Ridley Scott, *Alien*, in which the alien that hijacks a space crew gestates within a human host (I'll stop painting the picture here so as not to horrify my dear reader into putting this book down). Although the state of pregnancy can seem like futuristic science fiction, to me it's even scarier that all too often, it firmly ensconces women into a limited position within the historical patriarchy. Gender equity seems achievable, and then one need only to become pregnant to realize how much more progress needs to be made.

For the first 3 decades of my life, I naively thought that gender equity as related to women and men was already our collective reality. All throughout my medical education years and clinical training, the top students and physicians-in-training among my peers included both women and men. I looked around and saw equity and parity. I didn't spend much time worrying about how I would balance my future as a physician with my years-long wish to have 4 children of my own.

As a history major in college my first year on campus, I somehow managed to pull a top number in the class registration lottery and scored a spot in a small, cozy 15-student freshman seminar entitled "America in the 1960s." Included in the course reading syllabus was Betty Friedan's *The Feminine Mystique*, originally published in 1963. In this now landmark book, Friedan outlined "the problem that had no name": even college-educated women left their education and careers for lives as housewives and mothers, yet despite this "choice," they were unhappy and unsatisfied. Here I was, at 18 years old, looking at the issue of inequity in the household division of labor as (literally) a subject matter in my history books. So this was history, right? Had we already evolved past this inequity?

Especially by the time I was in medical school, any questions about work-life balance seemed quaint and I continued to naively believe that inequity was a matter of historical significance, not our world's current state of affairs. Of course I would figure out working parenthood; parity in a partnership, raising a family, and running a household all made good common sense. I was in for a big wake-up call. My 4 kids were born over 2002 to 2006, and despite the calendar telling me it was the 21st century, my maternity leave and child care were anything but equitable.

My first pregnancy went smoothly overall, but because of some issues, I did require precautionary weekly ultrasounds and stress tests in the third trimester. At the time, I thought that juggling those weekly appointments with my rigorous pediatrics residency work hours was challenging, but that was a breeze compared with navigating my second pregnancy with identical twins, or, as I like to call it, the best 2-for-1 deal ever. But I digress; for the first pregnancy, the kid hadn't even showed up yet, but the disproportionate time investment between the 2 parents to care for this as-of-yet-born life had already begun. Make no mistake: I was thrilled and eager to meet this child, but I didn't yet realize that the unpaid labor of motherhood had already begun with those weekly obstetric appointments. His father, in an equally demanding medical training program, wasn't supported by the system to take the time to help the mother of his child at the numerous required prenatal visits and testing. Even before the child was born, the unpaid labor of caring for the child was already quite unbalanced between the parents. Sadly, this phenomenon is a factor that sets the stage for inequity once the child is born.

Those who feel that gender equity, particularly in female-male partnerships, is a pipe dream may shrug their shoulders at this point and say "Oh well, it's genetic, so of course the mothers should be more involved in child-rearing, as they are the child bearers." I'd argue, however, that parenting means so much more than mere anatomy and logistics. It is true that some realms (carrying the pregnancy and breastfeeding, although I can't think of much else) are going to be 98:2 tasks. But other tasks will be 50:50; some, 30:70; and some, 70:30. If there is a domain that is 98:2, then please, partners, step up and balance out the other domains. We will delve more into these domains as part of our greater road map analogy, but as just one quick example: for a newborn's overnight feedings, even if the baby takes breast milk, dads can feed the baby pumped breast milk, or be the one in charge of changing the diapers.

START A CONVERSATION

Pregnancy is an ideal time for partners to have conversations about both the big picture and all the little details that will eventually add up to the big picture. As partners, what are your global, overarching goals for your son? What are the daily aspects of your family's life, and your son's, that will coalesce to form an existence, a framework to achieve the nurture part of the nature-nurture (genetic-environmental) influence on human development? It's OK to not have all the answers and ideas from the onset. Your road map will include twists and turns, and you'll need to pivot as you learn which strategies are effective and which strategies require a "reroute" of reexamination and tweaking. That's why we are having these conversations. And, to be fully honest, these are the conversations I wish I took part in with my partner more frequently when I was welcoming my own babies to our family at the start of the 21st century.

Let's have more conversations about our mindset and our goals for our sons starting in pregnancy. As I type this, I imagine my own 3 sons in their futures, should they choose to become parents: I want them to be equal, active participants. Men shouldn't be bystanders in the process of welcoming a new child to the family. Let's make sure men have an equitable stake in this process. They may not be able to carry a fetus or breastfeed, but these 2 tasks are not how parenthood is defined. My hope for my sons, and for all male partners, is that they are able to participate and have a stake in the full human experience of the myriad, countless aspects of parenthood.

Gender Expectations Conversation

Many pregnancies include a 20-week prenatal ultrasound, or anatomical scan, to assess the growth and development of the fetus, measure the size of critical organs such as the heart and brain, and ensure that the pregnancy is progressing according to plan. To be clear, this is a *medical* imaging study to ensure the fetus' and birthing parent's health and to make sure that the pregnancy is progressing smoothly. That said, in the United States, it also happens to be an opportunity to find out the assigned sex of the baby.

Most sources indicate that the majority of parents-to-be wish to learn the sex of their baby before birth. Often this decision is based on pure curiosity or logistics, but I find the issue interesting. Full disclosure: I'm "that person" on social media when expectant parents share the sex of their baby before birth; I personally comment along the lines of "So happy to hear that the pregnancy is progressing healthfully and that all the organs are the correct sizes in the correct places!" Yes, this is my passive-aggressive, not-so-subtle reminder of the true reason for the imaging. The prenatal ultrasound's purpose is not to determine the shopping list or a nursery color scheme. It boggles the mind to consider the evolution of medicine in just this century and realize what a modern issue it is to have the ability to determine the child's sex assignment before birth. It must also be stated that we as a society have learned a lot about the spectrum of gender and that the sex assigned at birth may not match the gender identity of an individual as they get older. For all these reasons, the persistence of the cultural preoccupation with the sex assignment is vexing.

Parenthood is the ultimate journey, and everyone's road map will look different and will evolve as time passes and their son grows. It makes sense from an existential standpoint that many of us parents-to-be wish to partake in a kind of illusion that we have some semblance of control over an uncontrollable situation by finding out "what" we are going to have: a boy or a girl. And to be clear, I don't begrudge us the ability to plan ahead and prepare both mentally and logistically. It's what we *do* with the information of the sex of the baby that matters, because when you really think about it, knowing the sex of the baby shouldn't really change a whole lot, right?

THE FAMILY JOURNEY

Craft Your Road Map

Every family looks different and has a unique structure and requires distinct needs. Some will be 2-parent families, 1-parent households, or those with or without intergenerational support. However unique, you will all need to examine your goals and needs and adjust your road map accordingly. We will outline tasks that require discussion and planning to not only share the workload equitably but also model for our sons what it looks like to be a full partner and parent.

A family I spoke with about this issue (at the time of this writing, the family had a grade school girl, a preschool boy, and a toddler boy) pointed out how even before birth, so many behaviors and interests are already attributed to a child once the sex is determined. This mom voiced concerns over T-shirts that read "Boy Mom," "Girl Mom," etc. She told me "We don't raise our kids by gender, we raise them by interest." Dad chimed in that as a male parent expecting a daughter, he felt an implication that he "wouldn't know what to do with a girl," and he wondered aloud, "How could it possibly be different to spend time with a girl versus a boy?" Mindset is everything: Mom stated, "I'm not having a girl, I'm having a kid." And once their daughter was born, her mindset was "It's not a girl; rather, I have a Sophie." Her child is not her sex; she is a person, a little human, with the full array of human characteristics.

A dad I spoke with who had a daughter followed by a son was struck by the hearty congratulations he received from coworkers, family members, and neighbors at the news of the pregnancy with the son. He was baffled by the frequently encountered sense that a man should be elated to be expecting a boy, as if now his life and legacy were complete. He said of the matter, "I'm not the king of England!" Why do we, in the 21st century, perpetuate this groupthink that the family lineage is fostered only by sons? It's clearly a larger issue than just preserving the family name. On the note of family surnames, there are many ways to tackle that issue.

My wonderful sister-in-law of 2 decades is one of 3 daughters, with no sons. When she married my brother, she had quite a few reasons to keep her maiden name, one of those being to ensure that her family surname would continue.

On the subject of names, including last names, many women don't take their partner's last name, or alternatively, they choose to hyphenate. Many grapple with the decision and might reluctantly take their partner's last name because they want to share their children's last name. A parent I spoke with found the amount of patriarchy found within the issue of children's names staggering. This mother, who did not adopt her partner's last name, chose to give both her kids *her* last name. She heard many questions from relatives, teachers, and even strangers for years afterward. Incredible that a mere shift in naming strategy can ruffle so many feathers.

The Division of Household Labor Conversation

Any relationship, and any partnership, benefits from communication. The clearer the expectations, the better. Pregnancy is an ideal time to have conversations about the division of labor within the household, both before and after the new baby arrives. Any journey begins with an itinerary or a road map, yes? Similarly, partners should sit together and create a metaphorical road map for the family transition and the arrival of their son.

This road map should include not just necessary manual tasks, such as housecleaning, laundry, and yard work, but also the mental load of keeping track of doctor appointments, shopping lists, dates of when the crib will be delivered, and more. All too often, the mental load of what needs to be done, when, and how falls to the female partner in a female-male partnership, leading to frustration, stress, and inequity. The default setting is that the female partner handles these jobs and all the details that go along with them, so partners need to have these conversations with awareness and intention.

Will this early draft, or road map, of the division of labor be carved in stone? Absolutely not. Parenthood in general requires the ability to stop and change directions, to reevaluate the route, to recognize what is and is not working, and to adjust accordingly. Every kid is different, every parent is different, and, on top of each difference, new circumstances will arise that shift the dynamic.

Your road map will be fluid; think of it as water in a rushing current of a river, ebbing and flowing. Keep the successful strategies, and reevaluate the tricky patches. Moving, new careers, family illness, and the arrival of another child, as just a few examples, will all shift the balance. A silver lining of the COVID-19 pandemic is that we've all (I hope) learned to pivot and be more flexible. We would be wise to maintain this *growth* mindset and discard any *fixed* mindset.

THE FAMILY JOURNEY

Plot Your Route

Even during pregnancy, partners are wise to discuss the daily, weekly, monthly, and big-picture tasks that comprise running a household and raising children. Discuss specific chores, who will do what, and, more importantly, who will do the mental work of planning for and executing said chores (it's not enough to require reminders from a partner).

Some *daily* chores to start the conversation include

- Preparing meals
- Washing dishes, loading/unloading the dishwasher
- Tidying up
- Taking out garbage/emptying the diaper pail
- Running errands

In the morning,

- Doing early morning wake-ups (after 4:00 am)
- Changing diapers, dressing the baby
- Feeding the baby
- Preparing bottles, pumped breast milk, or formula for child care
- Packing a daily bag for child care
- Doing child care drop-off or sitter transition

In the evening,

- Doing child care pickup or sitter transition
- Changing diapers

- Feeding the baby
- Managing the nighttime bath
- Managing the bedtime routine
- Washing bottles and breast pump components
- Doing the overnight shift (until 4:00 am)

Continue reading for weekly, monthly, and big-picture details to discuss with your family.

In *Harry Potter and the Goblet of Fire,* we learn that the magical feasts of Hogwarts, the wizarding school, are prepared by the castle house elves, who also surreptitiously clean and keep the facility running at an efficient clip. What is particularly notable about the house elves is that these essential, castle-running tasks are performed with near-zero awareness of even the existence of house elves until Hermione initiates an awareness campaign on behalf of the elves' rights. I've thought about the Hogwarts house elves frequently over the years. There was something that sounded familiar about keeping a complex organization humming along with little-to-no awareness of the day-to-day, minute-to-minute details that keep the ship afloat. How exactly do birthday gifts magically appear, toilet paper rolls remain in stock, or dental appointments get made 6 months ahead of time?

The Division of Emotional Labor Conversation

Eve Rodsky's 2019 book *Fair Play,* which Reese Witherspoon facilitated turning into a documentary in 2022, examines the *emotional* labor of running a household. Pre-children, Rodsky writes that as a couple, she and her husband had a dynamic that was equitable, but everything changed once babies arrived, causing her as a mother to become the "default parent." She writes:

> Because Seth and I hadn't pre-negotiated how to share in the domestic workload before Zach [their first child] came along, it defaulted to me. He'd leave for work in the office, and I'd spend the next eight hours boiling bottles, doing dishes, folding laundry, restocking the nursery, running to the grocery store, picking up prescriptions, preparing meals, tidying up, *and* entertaining and attending to my little one.

Rodsky points out that her system to promote parity in household mental and physical tasks doesn't benefit just female partners in female-male partnerships; both partners will have happier, healthier relationships. "Almost every man interviewed in connection with this project said nagging is what they hate most about being married, but they also admit that they wait for their wives to tell them what to do at home."[1] Of course, if the task was handled in a timely manner in the first place, "nagging" would not occur. Ownership over the parity benefits each partner, as well as benefits the relationship as a whole.

THE FAMILY JOURNEY

Taking Turns Behind the Wheel

The division of labor can be challenging for parents who have experienced absence or death of a partner or who have gone through separation or divorce from a partner. That said, single parents and co-parents do not have to go it alone. Here are some ideas and questions that may ease your planning.

Ideas for single parents to consider that may reduce household and mental labor

Marika Lindholm, the founder of Empowering Solo Moms Everywhere (https://esme.com), has shared some single-parent solutions she has observed.

- Share a home or rental with close family or with another single parent you trust or meet, such as through a local single-parents group.
- Explore night shifts, flextime, or part-time work.

---

1. Rodsky E. *Fair Play: A Game-changing Solution for When You Have Too Much to Do (and More Life to Live)*. Putnam; 2019.

- Build a face-to-face and virtual support network to create awareness of trusted sitters, effective after-school programs, and newer or littler-known programs.
- Participate in carpooling or food, child care, or clothing exchanges.[2]

Questions for co-parents to consider that may reduce custody-related mental labor

In the American Academy of Pediatrics book *Co-parenting Through Separation and Divorce*, pediatrician David L. Hill, MD, FAAP, and child custody mediator Jan Blackstone, PsyD, have shared questions, as well as guidance, for co-parents to establish a schedule through which they share their child's time.

- How long have the parents been apart?
- How have the parents been sharing the children's time to date?
  - Is there currently, or does there need to be, a primary caregiver? If so, which parent is most likely to share the children's time and foster a relationship with the other parent?
  - What is the distance each parent must travel to exchange the children?
    - Are there any barriers to exchanges—for example, restraining orders or orders of protection that prevent the parents from interacting?
    - Extracurricular activities?
  - What is each parent's work schedule?
  - What is the age of each child?
  - Does any child have [functional] needs [for a disability]?[3]

Importantly, through the 2020 Single Mom Income and Time-Sharing Survey, journalist Emma Johnson found that equally shared parenting time correlated with higher incomes for single mothers (www.wealthysinglemommy.com/survey). In other words, when it's safe for co-parents to pursue equal physical custody, it may narrow the gender pay gap[4] and model greater gender equity for their son.

2. Ideas derived from Lindholm M. Creative strategies from single parents on juggling work and family. *Harvard Business Review*. April 8, 2021. Accessed May 16, 2023. https:/hbr.org/2021/04/creative-strategies-from-single-parents-on-juggling-work-and-family.
3. Questions reproduced from Parenting plans. In: Blackstone J, Hill DL. *Co-parenting Through Separation and Divorce: Putting Your Children First*. American Academy of Pediatrics; 2020:149.
4. The gender pay gap is an inequity in how employed women and men are paid. Globally, because of discrimination against women in the workplace, women are paid about 20% less than men (https://news.un.org/en/story/2022/09/1126901).

One family I spoke with, who at the time of our discussion had a grade schooler, a preschooler, and a toddler, said that both partners cook, and when it comes to household tasks, "whoever cares about the issue more handles it," which has proven to be a good balance for them. Recognize what is and is not working, and keep your "script" flexible.

THE FAMILY JOURNEY

Must-see Destinations on Your Road Map

Pregnancy discussions should include *weekly* chores needed to keep a household running. Some ideas to spark your conversation and your division of labor planning can include

- Planning meals
- Shopping for food
- Laundering clothing
- Changing and laundering bed linens
- Doing dry cleaning drop-off and pickup
- Vacuuming
- Cleaning the kitchen, cleaning the bathroom(s)
- Dusting
- Managing trash and recycling
- Sorting mail
- Watering plants
- Doing yard work
- Self-care, exercise time for each partner

Have a conversation about dividing this labor equally. Maybe the plan you've decided on together requires you to trade off certain chores every week. People get sick, work schedules change, and, sometimes, chores are forgotten. Don't let the frustration of extra chores being on your list go unexpressed. Talk with your partner.

Over the past several years when discussing gender issues within the home with the families I care for in my clinical pediatrics practice, I have increasingly used terms such as *unpaid labor, the mental load,* and *cognitive labor.* If I had a penny for every time a patient's mom tells me "I'm not working right now" or "I left my job"… I am always quick to pipe in with the clarification that parenthood is the most important and significant work, or "job," we can do, and its value should not be diminished simply because it's unpaid work. It's a huge example of very important work, so vital to our society, that happens to be unpaid labor.

Our list of household chores and our grocery-shopping lists may not acknowledge the entirety of the mental load. Kate Mangino addresses the concept of cognitive labor in her book, *Equal Partners,* by sharing a story from her own experiences that describes enrolling her daughter in music lessons. In kindergarten, her daughter expressed an interest in music. Anticipating the need for musical instruction; having conversations to decide which instrument; researching local music schools versus private teachers; comparing prices, schedules, and compatibility with the family schedule; paying for, and driving to and from, lessons; and continually evaluating progress and relationship with the music instructor all add up as cognitive labor tasks that may not be listed on a chore list, yet they are still time consuming and very important.

Artist and graphic designer Mary Catherine Starr shares thoughtful and often funny takes on the gender balance of the household in her Instagram page, momlife_comics. In June 2022, she posted a series of images, 5 Lies the Patriarchy Tells Us About Our Male Partners, and concluded with this powerful statement: "Women will not be equal until they are free from the weight of unpaid domestic labor. Our male partners can do their part to move us toward equality by taking on an equal amount of the household labor (and mental labor) of parenting."[5]

---

5. @momlife_comics. 5 lies the patriarchy tells us about our male partners. June 2022. https://www.instagram.com.

THE FAMILY JOURNEY

Must-see Destinations Along Your Road Map Route

Discussions between partners to equitably divide the mental labor of raising a son and running a household should include *monthly* chores, such as

- Paying bills, balancing the checkbook
- Managing health insurance/health spending accounts
- Managing investments
- Bulk shopping (eg, diapers, wipes, paper towels)
- Scheduling and attending pediatric appointments
- Maintaining the car
- Managing or hiring services for home improvements or repairs
- Planning family outings/weekends
- Finding/coordinating sitters
- Cleaning the refrigerator

Yearly, big-picture tasks to divide between partners can include

- Planning travel
- Planning vacations
- Arranging holiday, birthday, or special occasion gatherings

The outdated notion that the man in a female-male partnership is the financial breadwinner—therefore, the woman should bear the brunt of household chores—doesn't even hold up when the woman earns more than the man. A 2022 study from the University of Bath showed that moms who outearned dads' salaries still did more of the housework. Even worse, especially among married couples, the more the mom earned, paradoxically, the more housework she took on. Study author Joanna Syrda, PhD, said of this finding:

> Married couples that fail to replicate the traditional division of income may be perceived—both by themselves and others—to be deviating from the norm. What may be happening is that, when men earn less than women, couples neutralize this by increasing traditionality through housework—in

other words, wives do more and husbands do less as they try to offset this 'abnormal' situation by leaning into other conventional gender norms.[6]

I point this out as part of our larger conversation with ourselves and with our partners, to promote self-awareness and to mindfully prevent falling into patterns that do not promote our greater goals.

THE FAMILY JOURNEY

Roadblock Ahead

Are you familiar with the term *strategic incompetence* (alternatively known as *weaponized incompetence* or *feigned incompetence*)? In necessary household tasks, a partner may blatantly state incapability (or seem incapable) of completing a particular task, resulting in that task becoming the responsibility of someone else, typically the "default parent." This scenario often innocently appears as a single scenario, but the imbalance moves forward from that point relative to that particular task, sticking forevermore like permanent Velcro to be "just how it is." The task may become the complete responsibility of the female partner, or it's possible that the male partner will tackle the task yet require an inordinate amount of supervision and guidance.

An example of requiring excessive guidance could involve grocery shopping. Imagine a meticulous list made by the female partner for the male partner, not only itemized in the order in which one moves through the store but also visualized with photos or helpful notes attached. Certainly, grown-ups can figure out how to buy apples and milk without extensive hand-holding or instruction. But if a partner takes a passive-aggressive "I'm not good at that" stance, the result may be that the other partner simply takes over the task because "it's just easier this way." Somewhat more concerning is that moving forward, somehow the task may not ever again be expected of the "incompetent" partner.

(continued on next page)

---

6. Pahr K. Study shows moms who earn more than dads do more of the housework. Fatherly. April 1, 2022. Accessed May 16, 2023. https://www.fatherly.com/news/study-shows-that-moms-who-earn-more-than-dads-do-more-of-the-housework.

How to navigate this roadblock

An approach to prevent strategic incompetence is to verbally own up to strengths and weaknesses and to use this list to strategize who does what. If something doesn't fit a partner's skill set, fine, but the question must be asked, what *other* task can they then shoulder, or assume responsibility for, to maintain equity in the home? This conversation needs to be open and honest and to not fall prey to the idea of gendered skill sets. Men can be excellent cooks (consider the prevalence of male executive chefs), and women can enjoy yard work or car maintenance.

INTERACTIONS WITH EXTENDED FAMILY OR THE GREATER COMMUNITY

Does finding out whether you're having "a boy" or "a girl" alter your mindset and expectations for what your future family, your parenting journey, will look like? Of course it does; that is human nature. As a society, we've learned a lot about gender norms over the decades. We now recognize those individuals who are gender fluid or nonbinary. It is now well established that the assigned sex at birth, whether female or male, doesn't mean an individual's gender identity will match as they become older. Our expectations are partly due to decades of patriarchy, embedded in our subconscious, even if we consider ourselves forward thinking and enlightened. Many people take issue with the #boymom hashtag because this tends to perpetuate stereotypes, give excuses for "boys will be boys" behaviors, and work at odds with gender equity.

Our identity as individuals is not defined by our gender. We are people, humans, first and foremost. A dear lifelong friend of mine's younger child who was assigned female at birth has come out as nonbinary, using the pronouns *they/them/theirs*. This has been an adjustment for the entire family, especially their mother. As open-minded and accepting as my friend is (her professional career, in fact, supports and involves the care of tweens and teens who are defining who they truly are, despite sex assigned at birth), her path has included the process of grieving the lost expectations of having a "daughter" and all that would entail. I share this story as a reminder that our sons, and our children, are not solely defined by their sex assigned at birth.

During your pregnancy, should you choose to find out the sex of your baby and to share the information with family and friends, you'll start to notice some generational and societal expectations embedded within the comments and questions from others. There will be a prevalent perception if you tell people you're expecting a son, "Oh, boys are so easy." (Birthing 3 sons within 18 months, I wish I had a penny for every time someone told me this, ranging from complete strangers, to family members, to everyone in between.) Does the sentiment that "boys are so easy" perpetuate unhelpful patterns of communication? Why is it so common that we don't expect to talk with, and learn from, our sons, in the way we do our daughters? Shouldn't we *want* our sons to express themselves fully to us? Isn't this part of raising a human? Communicating with our kids (boy *or* girl *or* kid), building a relationship, and helping them acquire the skills to form their own relationships and navigate their way forward?

THE FAMILY JOURNEY

A Bump in the Road

In the excitement of pregnancy, despite our best intentions, we ourselves may fall prey to society's expectations for what our future sons will be. Self-reflect, show yourself grace, and reframe these situations as teachable moments, knowing that with intention, we are still moving the needle toward greater gender equity.

The theme here is to be careful about expectations and plans for your son, even as early as your pregnancy. When we bring a new human into the world, they are an individual to be loved and supported. All too often, we bestow our own experiences, dreams, and goals on our child. One family I spoke with who was expecting a son after their firstborn daughter was told by the grandfather "Now I have someone to take fishing with me." Why can't daughters go fishing? What if your son doesn't like fishing? Of course, this grandfather is excited about the prospect of the new grandchild and is planning aloud how the two will bond and spend time together, which is fantastic. And this doesn't necessarily need to be verbally squashed by us parents when these conversations come up. What I would gently suggest, however, is that when the child is 6 years old and there's a pressure to go fishing, sure, give it a try, but be your child's ally and support their own consent and choices and follow their lead whether they want to participate in this activity or not.

THE DECISION TO EXPAND FAMILY AS RELATED TO GENDER EXPECTATIONS

A few families I spoke with commented on how gender can influence the decision to expand a family. Society sure loves a matched set: "A boy and a girl." When my kids were younger and passerby saw 3 older brothers and the youngest, a girl, the overwhelming comment was "Oh, you got your girl." To be clear, I was sure I was incapable of creating a girl. I also happen to come from a very boy-proportioned family: my dad is one of 5 boys, with no girls; my mom has only a brother, with no sisters; and I have 2 older brothers, with no sisters. I honestly wasn't even sure what I would do with a girl. I wanted another human, another kid, no matter who this person was. And frankly, my daughter has been such a strong force for her entire life that she defies all stereotypes of all that was supposed to bring pink and sparkles and tulle and other such conventions into our lives. I was fully prepared for 4 boys; how would the fact that she is a girl dictate who she is as an individual person? Those who had thought tea parties and dolls were finally going to happen for me were disappointed to hear that I enjoy all 4 kids' eclectic tastes, which, frankly, do not run along gender lines.

One family in my clinical practice shared with me that once they had a daughter followed by a son, everyone told them "Oh, now you're done," even vocally expressing surprise when they planned for a third pregnancy and child. A friend who has 4 daughters is incredulous that for years, random people out and about would feel the need to tell their father "I feel so sorry for you." Really? For one thing, what kind of message does that send the daughters, who are very much listening to this conversation? For another, these girls (at the time of this writing, out of college, in college, and in high school) are academic achievers and athletes, with the oldest now serving in the military, defying the stereotypes of what it means to "be a girl."

Let's not assume what it means when we meet kids of specific genders, and as parents, let's not put on our kids, specifically our sons, what they can and cannot do because of their assigned sex at birth. Our kids are so much more than their assigned sex at birth.

CRAFTING A PARENTING PLAN

Pregnancy is an odd time. You may find out your expected due date and feel that it seems so far off and that you have plenty of time to prepare. Don't be fooled. The "due date" (I even chuckle as I type those words) is but a mere *estimate* of when you'll deliver: the 40-week gestation mark. Trust me, a baby's birth isn't like placing an online order with a guaranteed delivery date. A full-term pregnancy is anywhere from 37 weeks to 42 weeks; that's more than a month's range of possible birth dates, assuming the baby makes it to full-term pregnancy. And certainly, babies are born early quite frequently.

That is to say, it's never too soon to have parenting discussions on the topic of work schedules, planned parental leave, and contingency plans for when (not if!) your child gets sick. A silver lining of the pandemic is that the great push to remote work in 2020 meant that even for industries that have been historically inflexible, lo and behold, new ways to work efficiently and effectively, while being present for one's family, are entirely possible. (Readers, please also refer to Chapter 3, Nurturing Infants to Be Better Men, for more information on leave options.) Partners should have conversations early and often about what degree of workplace flexibility each will have once their baby arrives.

You'll share the news of the pregnancy to your inner circles first. When you've decided to share the news of it with your respective workplaces, that is the perfect time to inquire about options available to you in *each partner's* workplace. Parental leave, flextime, and work-from-home possibilities should be explored. Plenty of families use the significant life transition of a new child's arrival as a catalyst for life changes they've already considered making. The plan should be flexible because that's how life and parenthood work, but examine which strategies could work and which may not work, and make decisions from there.

Discussing workplace flexibility with your employer can be daunting. You can propose to your workplace an initial trial time of a month or two to make sure the flexible plan is working for all parties. If a work colleague

THE FAMILY JOURNEY

Plot Your Road Map Course

Investigate all options for parental leave. Whether you work for a larger corporation with formalized options or for a smaller business, work creatively with your partner and employer to craft a plan that is right for you and your son. As just one example, a family I care for in my clinical practice has 2 educator parents. They chose to take leave sequentially, so their son was home with one parent for a stretch, and when that parent went back to the workplace, the other partner was the stay-at-home parent with protected leave time. Find the solution that works best for your family.

is using a desirable flexible schedule, cite their circumstance as an example. Point out that your employer's goals are best met by productive employees who can operate at their best. Be ready with specifics to your plan: schedule, accessibility, and collaborating with coworkers.

The United States is one of the few countries in the world to not mandate federal paid family leave. The issue is clearly systemic. theSkimm has shared a list of 500 companies that *do* have paid family-leave policies, and it continues to gather information with the hashtag #ShowUsYourLeave database. theSkimm shares that it offers its own employees 18 weeks of paid leave, including for adoption, fostering, and surrogacy.[7] Approximately 90% of US workers have access to unpaid family leave, whereas only about a quarter have access to paid family leave. Women take longer leaves than men: 54 days versus 18 days for a new child.[8]

7. Skimm impact: paid family leave. theSkimm. Accessed May 17, 2023. https://www.theskimm.com/paid-family-leave-benefits.
8. Herr J, Roy R, Klerman JA, Abt Associates Inc. *Gender Differences in Needing and Taking Leave.* Chief Evaluation Office, US Dept of Labor; 2020. https://www.dol.gov/sites/dolgov/files/OASP/evaluation/pdf/WHD_FMLAGenderShortPaper_January2021.pdf.

When dads in female-male partnerships take family leave, there are mental health benefits for dads and moms. "The postpartum period is supposed to be this beautiful time where you celebrate your new little one. And unfortunately, it goes unnoticed that many folks struggled during this time. They have a change of their identity and responsibility... there's a strain on the interpersonal relationship between the partners," states Jenn Leiferman, director with the Colorado School of Public Health and author of a study on how dads experience prenatal and postpartum anxiety.[9] Fathers taking advantage of parental leave helps the family, as well as serves as a buffer for depression and anxiety.

Gender Reveal

I was born in the '70s. My kids were born in the early/mid-2000s. I remember getting a digital camera early in my first pregnancy when they were still considered new because I wanted to get used to the technology before my first son was born. With digital photos, social media began to rise; MySpace hit 1 million monthly users around 2004. I think about this a lot because every day in my clinic, I personally cannot imagine parenting in the social media age. It was stressful enough observing one of my identical twins mastering a new developmental milestone well before his brother. I don't envy parents who face the current pressure of logging onto social media and seeing babies their own kids' ages doing things that their own kids (and family) may or may not be doing yet. The pressure to post the top 1% of our lives is real, yet ironically, these posts don't reflect the full nature of our textured, real, complete lives.

You can probably draw a straight line between the prevalence of social media and gender-reveal parties. It seems that *all* life events have been amped up for the sake of social media announcements. Some uncontrolled fires in the western portion of the United States have been directly linked to gender-reveal parties gone amiss. In 2020, a "smoke-generating pyro-technic device" ignited a wildfire that tore through thousands of acres east of Los Angeles.[10] As with so many aspects of parenthood, the societal

---

9. Parker H, Murray B, Valenski A. The benefits (for the whole family) when dads take family leave. theSkimm. June 16, 2022. Accessed May 17, 2023. https://www.theskimm.com/parenting/benefits-family-when-dads-take-family-leave.

10. Morales C, Waller A. A gender-reveal celebration is blamed for a wildfire: it isn't the first time. *New York Times.* September 7, 2020. Accessed May 17, 2023. https://www.nytimes.com/2020/09/07/us/gender-reveal-party-wildfire.html.

trend to up the ante for gender reveals is arguably unnecessary, anxiety producing, and, in some cases, literally dangerous.

As a mom and a pediatrician, I take issue with the overt emphasis on the assigned sex of the child and the resultant tendency for family and friends to regard this new child, full of potential, as limited by how society traditionally defines genders. I know I may seem like a stick-in-the-mud to some with this stance, but perhaps there's a way we can celebrate this new child without putting them into a box of expectations before they are even born. Also, note that "gender reveal" is a misnomer; what's revealed is the sex assigned at birth. Do parents indeed want to throw a party focused on something as personal as their child's reproductive parts?

Michael Ian Black wrote of his first child:

> As soon as you were born, the first thing the doctor did was announce to us your sex. 'It's a boy,' she said. In that first moment—after all the anticipation, all the guessing and name-picking and speculation—the fact of your boyness felt trivial, inconsequential. There you were, our child, our baby. What difference did your sex make? None, as far as I could tell. That's what I would have said if somebody had asked in the moment, but now I feel like that's not true.[11]

We are better served to think of our child as having endless potential and to be mindful of societal expectations that limit opportunities.

Gender Considerations When Preparing the Nest

Simple is best. It's a great life motto, and it's an even better theme when the birth of a child is imminent. When preparing for your new son, remember that less is more. Babies really need only a few things: something to eat (breast milk or formula), something to pee and poop into (diapers), a safe place to sleep (a crib that meets current safety standards), and a safe way to ride in the car (a rear-facing infant car safety seat). Everything else is bells and whistles. As a mom of 4 close-in-age kids, including twins, I can state that keeping life simple helped me retain my sanity as a parent. Don't make life harder than it already is! A key part of this strategy is to realize how quickly parenthood evolves. Your infant will constantly grow and develop; what he needs at 1 month of age will change drastically by the time he is 5 months old and again when he is 9 months old.

---

11. Black MI. *A Better Man: A (Mostly Serious) Letter to My Son.* Algonquin Books of Chapel Hill; 2020.

Simple is best, yet the baby product marketing juggernaut wants your money and will happily provide lengthy "must-have" baby registry lists. Parents are wise to regard this marketing phenomenon with their eyes wide open. Especially if you are expecting your first child, the options are overwhelming, and in your anxiety to properly prepare, you may overbuy. Borrow what you can, buy items secondhand, consider online Freecycle or Buy Nothing groups, and ensure that any baby equipment meets current safety standards by visiting the US Consumer Product Safety Commission (www.cpsc.gov).

During pregnancy, be mindful of where you obtain infant and child care health and parenting information, and make sure each partner takes time to educate themselves on the forthcoming tasks of parenthood. Understand that internet searches on a particular subject will prioritize paid advertisers over quality content and won't be your best source of information. Both partners can and should explore parenting resources to prepare for their child's arrival; both parents should have a working knowledge of basic health issues to keep their child care equitable. Beware of the tendency for one parent to become a gatekeeping, default parent who knows more health and safety information than the other. A parent I spoke with discussed the challenges of taking on the mental load of being the keeper of this information, and then circumstances would arise with the child that led her to convince her partner that they needed to act, leading to arguments and conflict.

THE FAMILY JOURNEY

Supplies for the Road

The baby product marketing juggernaut would have us believe that infants require oodles of products, and this is simply not the case. After obtaining the essentials, remember that the rest are bells and whistles. Keeping things simple not only helps your budget but also helps prevent possible gender-stereotype pitfalls.

Diaper bags have come a long way, so it'll be easy to find options that *both* parents can use. Many of the families I care for in my practice simply use a backpack; one mom recently told me how all the hundreds of pockets in most diaper bags that are currently for sale stress her out. Look for options that both parents can use, easily grabbed on your way out the door for your baby's 4-month health supervision visit at the pediatrician's office.

There's a long-standing idea of the "mom bag," that women carry all things, "just in case." I have subscribed to this myself and have won that classic baby shower game of "Do you have this item in your bag?" more than once with all the random gear and stuff I've lugged around over the years. As it turns out, dads can carry supplies too... *Both* parents can transport necessary items on your journey.

After welcoming 3 sons, my kids' dad and I were on a budget, and necessity required that we not spend too much money for the fourth child, a daughter. You can take an educated guess at how many of her brothers' hand-me-downs she wore not only as an infant but also as the years went on. I remember a phase in which "boyfriend jeans" were trendy, so I chose to put that positive spin on the fact that my kindergarten daughter was wearing handed-down boy jeans. Star Wars gear was quite loved, regardless of gender. We saved money and, to boot, sent a gender-equal message to her and the rest of the world that you can show interest in whatever you like and wear whatever you like.

One family I spoke with knew their first was going to be a girl, so they went with animal themes for the nursery and the color green, which is her mom's favorite color. Mom said, "Definitely no onesies that said 'Daddy's Little Heartbreaker'!" Your surroundings support your mindset and set the stage. Be aware of this when preparing your nest, and save some money in the process.

In the era of social media, everything is amped up a bit, and this goes for nursery decor as well. Yet again, I must say I'm grateful my kids were born before social media really took off; our budget was very tight, and my kids' nurseries were pretty straightforward. We had the necessary essentials, but the rooms were definitely not Pinterest-worthy. In the grand scheme of things, did that matter? In the blink of an eye, your child is already transitioning to a big-kid bed, and the infant nursery already looks outdated. Be careful to not let idealized, created-for-social-media images of nurseries interfere with your family's choices, preferences, and reality-based budget. Going with gender-neutral colors and themes not only supports gender equity but also prepares you to repurpose items if you have more than one child.

Ultimately, preparing for the arrival of a new child is about meeting a new little person who will arrive with their own temperament and personality, with a whole world waiting for them. The baby registry list and nursery decor can be fun details for which to prepare, but ensure that your mindset is focused not on the material items involved in the care of an infant but rather on the anticipation of meeting this wonderful new person, filled with potential.

WORDS MATTER: PHRASES AT STAGES THAT DO US NO FAVORS

Language matters, and the words we use as we prepare for the arrival of a new baby influence not only our own mindset but also the patterns, choices, and outlook of our partners, family, friends, and community. Often words can become self-fulfilling prophecies. As a pediatrician, I hear the phrase "terrible twos" all the time in reference to the challenges of toddlers, yet toddlers are emerging individuals simply learning to navigate the world around them. If we repeatedly encounter the phrase "terrible twos," we internalize it to a certain degree; then we *expect* our child's third year after birth to be a challenging nightmare of sorts. Perception becomes reality. If you expect something to be awful, I guarantee you, it probably will be.

The same goes for the phrase "boys will be boys." If you choose to learn your child's sex before delivery, you'll undoubtedly encounter this phrase from anyone and everyone, even random shoppers in the grocery store (trust me on this one because I've lived it).

Unless both partners in a female-male partnership "help" run the home, please don't continue the generational habit of declaring men performing household tasks as "help." A male partner isn't helping; he's contributing to the teamwork of running a household. The debunking of the term *helping* that has long outworn its welcome is illustrated in a viral post that routinely makes the social media rounds. The post is entitled "I Don't Help My Wife."

I Don't Help My Wife

A friend came to my house for coffee, we sat and talked about life. At some point in the conversation, I said, "I'm going to wash the dishes and I'll be right back."

He looked at me as if I had told him I was going to build a space rocket. Then he said to me with admiration but a little perplexed: "I'm glad you help your wife, I do not help because when I do, my wife does not praise me. Last week I washed the floor and no thanks."

I went back to sit with him and explained that I did not "help" my wife. Actually, my wife does not need help, she needs a partner. I am a partner at home..., but it is not a "help" to do household chores.

I do not help my wife clean the house because I live here too and I need to clean it too.

I do not help my wife to cook because I also want to eat and I need to cook too.

I do not help my wife wash the dishes after eating because I also use those dishes.

Reproduced from Tee Edwards Facebook page. I don't help my wife. July 6, 2017. Accessed May 17, 2023. https://www.dailymail.co.uk/femail/article-4708974/Man-goes-viral-emotional-post-husband-duties.html.

The title alone is brilliant, isn't it? No wonder this photo-essay regularly makes the social media rounds; it grabs your attention because you're ready to be indignant yet the twist is that it illustrates what a true partnership looks like.

Your infant son will be here before you know it. From the early days in the hospital to the early weeks at home, he'll be learning lessons about love and connection daily. Teamwork and partnership will go a long way to not only nurture your son's future potential but also maintain your sanity and model gender equity for years to come. Whether cleaning a poopy diaper or soothing an infant son to sleep, fathers have much to offer. Everyone is better off when dads are consistently and equitably involved in their sons' lives.

RECOMMENDED RESOURCES FOR PARENTS AT THIS STAGE

Parker KT. *The Heart of a Boy: Celebrating the Strength and Spirit of Boyhood.* Workman Publishing; 2019. A photographic essay along the lines of *Humans of New York* that highlights a boy's preschool years through young adulthood, reflecting the fact that boys can be vulnerable, joyful, dedicated, playful, creative, resilient, expressive, independent, curious, and kind—and all these things at once. A great read when expecting a son to ensure you expand your mind and preconceived notions of what a boy can be.

Rodsky E. *Fair Play: A Game-changing Solution for When You Have Too Much to Do (and More Life to Live).* Putnam; 2019, and *Fair Play.* Documentary. Fair Play LLC; 2022. A book that is now a documentary, a modern look at the division of household labor of a dual working family that also examines the balance of unpaid, mental labor.

Chapter 3

Nurturing Infants to Be Better Men: Leading by Example With Equitable Teamwork, From Day One

Morgan Freeman's iconic, soothing voice narrates the 2005 feature-length nature documentary *March of the Penguins*, in which viewers witness the yearly journey and breeding rituals of the emperor penguins of Antarctica. The female penguins lay the egg; however, audiences may be surprised to learn that the egg is then carefully transferred to rest on the *male* penguin's feet, all the while shielding the egg from the harsh −80 °F (yes, that's 80 *below* zero) temperature. The *male* is then left to care for the penguin egg, while the female embarks on a precarious frozen journey to feed in the waters and retrieve food for the penguin chicks, 60 miles away. How fascinating to find that for some species, the role of the primary caregiver early in a newborn's life is, quite literally, assigned to the males.

Even within the human species, the idea of women "staying at home" to care for young children and the household is a relatively recent phenomenon, a product of the Industrial Age of the 1800s. For millennia, women served important, equal roles in both hunter-gatherer societies and, later, farming communities, providing food, clothing, and caregiving for their families. The gender roles within a household were quite equitable. Then, in the 1800s, a shift occurred. Whereas previously "work" would immediately provide for the family, after the shift, work would occur *outside* the home (eg, producing goods for a company and boss, in exchange for money to support the family). It was at this time that women's roles shifted to that of primary caregivers.

Fast-forward to the COVID-19 pandemic of the early 21st century. Waves of SARS-CoV-2 variants caused lockdowns and school closures and put families into a child care pinch. Although a silver lining for some families was a more flexible work arrangement, giving male parents the opportunity to get more involved with child care and household needs, all too often, the female parent was the parent who needed to pivot and adapt to shoulder, or assume the responsibilities of, the new pandemic landscape—whether to help kids with remote school or to help older grandparents. I must ask: Why are women's roles still caught in the outdated perception that women need to be the "default parent"? Why, when considering the history of several centuries, is the relatively recent phenomenon of women staying at home, as the nurturing members of our families, often regarded as "the way society has always been"? Why is a natural evolution or modification of out-dated, gender-lined structures regarded as (gasps, clutches pearl necklace) a potential threat to the fabric of society, especially in light of the fact that the current status quo structure is a relatively recent phenomenon? As a mother of 3 sons, I not only believe that men can be particularly nurturing, loving members of a family but have witnessed this firsthand. I also want my sons to experience the full range of humanity, including full parenthood, should they choose to become parents themselves one day.

MY THREE SONS

The spring season is a time of renewal and new beginnings. Appropriately, spring was the season in which I became a first-time parent, which you could say is the *ultimate* new beginning. Chicago weather in the spring is known for great variability; despite the brave tulips erupting from the earth, and bold magnolia trees blossoming, snow always falls in Chicago during the month of April. It usually melts within the day, but trust me, it's still snow. The birth of your first child is surreal under any circumstances, but the week that my oldest, a boy, was born, Chicago experienced temperatures in the 80s. My memories are neither hyperbole nor warped by nostalgia; it's more than 20 years later as I write this, and a quick internet search shows that his date of birth and the following few days continue to hold the records for high temperatures in Chicago for the month of April.

In this existentially surreal state, I brought my firstborn newborn home from the hospital. My main focus was ensuring survival (for him *and* me) and boosting my wimpy breast milk supply enough to sustain this new human life (spoiler alert: we both made it). In case you were wondering, being fully trained as a pediatrician does *not* make those early days of parenting a newborn baby any less scary.

Fast-forward 18 quick months later, and once again, I was postpartum, recovering in the mother-baby unit of my university hospital, this time having given birth to identical twin boys. The pediatrician who visited us to examine my sons after their birth walked into the room and straightaway asked me whether I planned on installing urinals in our bathrooms (In retrospect, honestly, that was a really good idea and a missed opportunity on my part!). In between humming the theme song for the 1960s American sitcom *My Three Sons* and juggling the daily tasks of running a household with 3 kids younger than 2 years, I was honestly operating in survival mode. My joke with the patients' families in my clinical pediatrics practice that are knee deep in raising young children continues to be "If everyone makes it to bedtime alive and fed, it's been a successful day!" And in those early, hazy months, that was my motto.

Beyond mere survival, though, thoughts toward my greater parenting goals began to percolate and surface. Becoming a mother to 3 boys in such a short amount of time woke something up within me. I distinctly remember that, even in the days following a prenatal ultrasound of my twins that confirmed we had 2 more boys on the way, I found my thoughts circling around the idea that if I were to be a mom to a brood of boys, by golly, these boys would be empathic, loving, considerate sons. Sixty-six percent of them hadn't even been born yet, and I was already hoping these little humans would amount to so much more than "a boy," would be so much more interesting than all the typical, narrow imagery that being a boy brings to mind. It was almost as if with the prospect of being outnumbered by gender 3 to 1, I was all the more determined to raise my boys as independently of societal and institutional gender expectations as I could. My sons would cook, they would be caregivers, and they would love; it shouldn't matter to us parents what society's at-times limited ideas of what a full man can be continue to perpetuate, especially notable in concepts such as "a man leaves his parents," when we know that the goal of raising daughters *and* sons is to raise functional adults, future members of society.

THE FAMILY JOURNEY

Each Mile Gets You to Your Destination

Newborns are born with inherent personality traits and temperament and then learn from their caregivers and the world around them. Starting off as somewhat of a blank slate, infants begin to absorb the messaging around them. What big-picture goals do you have for your son? Keeping these overarching goals at the back of your mind, guiding day-to-day decisions and role modeling, matters. Each little step comprises a big journey.

In the chaos of bringing a newborn home, the big-picture idea of promoting gender equity, especially when one parent has given birth and the other has not, may seem to be a modern problem, a luxury, or an obscure pipe dream. I would argue that baby steps in infancy (see what I did there?) promote equity in infant care, household tasks, and, in particular, father-son bonding and set the stage for years to come. Significant patterns are established in your son's infancy that will "stick," or persist into weeks, months, and, before you blink, years. A male penguin supporting a chick egg on his feet, a dad handling preschool drop-off, a father helping with sixth-grade homework while preparing dinner for the family—these fathers show that infancy is the time to set the stage for a progression. From birth to 5 years of age, children establish their self-esteem, identity, and ideas about gender roles within a family. The forming of connections between fathers and infants in early childhood creates an unbreakable bond, and *everyone* wins when our sons are raised with an awareness and promotion of gender equity.

AT THE HOSPITAL: SETTING THE STAGE

Childbirth, despite being the method by which we all begin our lives on earth, takes quite a toll on a mother's or birthing parent's body, whether a vaginal birth or a caesarean birth. As the mom recuperates and heals from the birth and works on breastfeeding during the critical early days of a newborn's life, these initial days, especially with the support and guidance of the hospital nurses, are an ideal opportunity to set the stage for strong involvement of the father or non-birthing parent. With lessons and demonstrations in bathing a newborn, comforting swaddle techniques, burping techniques after feedings, and diaper-changing strategies, even fathers or non-birthing parents who have had little or no prior experience with babies can gain the confidence to accomplish these very necessary caregiving tasks.

The daily infant care tasks of feeding, burping, diaper changes, swaddling, and bathing are not just mundane daily chores but wonderful opportunities for *connection* and for parent-infant bonding, for all parents. Decades of infant developmental research make it clear that a child's development from birth to 5 years is a critical life stage for children to learn how to connect with the humans around them, notably fathers, including how to socially interact with others and form relationships. The hardwiring of an infant's brain is molded and developed in these significant early days. A loving adult who attends to a baby's basic needs and responds to the baby's cries and early forms of communication lays significant groundwork for the baby to feel that they are loved, to know that they are valued, to develop self-esteem, and to learn about reciprocal relationships with the call and response. Yes, attending to a baby's needs is much, much more than mere child's play.

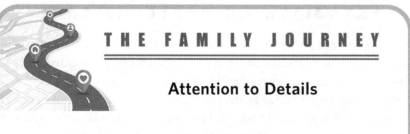

THE FAMILY JOURNEY

Attention to Details

Even a simple diaper change is an opportunity for connection with your infant son. Making eye contact with him, singing a song to him, smiling together, or responding to his cues all form the basis of self-esteem and the beginnings of a secure attachment between father and son.

I often joke with my patients' families that in our newborn stage, we humans are the neediest of all the animal species. In 2017, a giraffe at the New York Animal Adventure Park captured the attention of a national virtual audience while birthing her son; as a pediatrician of human babies, I had to laugh because after the giraffe calf was born, he was up and walking on his own within the hour. Human babies need anywhere from 9 months to 18 months to achieve this motor milestone! The fact that we as a species require a lot of "maintenance" as infants supports our social nature and interconnectedness with each other. The newborn period and infancy are a critical time to establish these early connections.

Infants have evolving visual abilities and see best at a feeding distance, typically 8 to 12 inches. I'm routinely asked as a pediatrician how to boost infant development in the early weeks after birth: time interacting with a loving caregiver, with a call and response, is priceless. All parents should put away distractions and screens and simply be present with your child, narrating or describing the day's events, even the watery poop you're cleaning off their bottom—it all counts! We're keeping it real, so communicating about your real lives, while they unfold in real time, is a perfect "conversation" topic. Birthing parents', non-birthing parents', dads', and moms' diverse ways of communication enrich a son's world. That you have 2 different styles, a diversity of styles, is not only OK but also a win for your son and his robust social-emotional development.

COMING HOME FROM THE HOSPITAL: ESTABLISHING PATTERNS EARLY

Moms who have given birth should focus on their medical recovery and should take the necessary steps to establish a healthy breastfeeding routine, if possible, which is no small feat in the first week after a newborn's birth. I recommend taking an overview, big-picture look at your necessary newborn and household tasks. When evaluating these necessary daily routines, many partners choose to divide the labor of caring for a newborn into input-output categories. Moms can handle the breastfeeding and then hand their newborn son off to the father or non-birthing parent for burping, upright time (to minimize the inevitable spit-ups), and diaper changes. Overnight awakenings can be handled either in a tag team approach, with both partners handling feedings and diaper changes at each wake-up, or with the choice to divide nocturnal labor into shifts, ensuring that each partner gets some uninterrupted sleeping time. Mom can handle awakenings and feedings until 2:00 am, for example, at which time Dad takes over bottle feedings of expressed breast milk or infant formula through the morning. This way, both partners are ensured a somewhat longer stretch of uninterrupted sleep.

THE FAMILY JOURNEY

Route Planning

Both partners will be tired with a young infant at home. There won't be a perfect day, but when you're both feeling relatively rested, sit together in person and have a conversation about how overnight feedings are being handled. Whether you split the night into shifts or reevaluate what it means to "have to work the next day" (Unpaid labor is still labor!), work toward equity. Alternatively, if the workload is shouldered more by one parent, the other parent should add responsibilities to their list. If your infant is older than 4 months and is overall healthy and gaining weight well, talk with his pediatrician about strategies to encourage longer stretches of sleep at night, as proper sleep is vital for *all* of your health.

Are dads as good as moms when soothing newborns? The answer is yes, and there are scientific data to back this assertion up. A Swedish study showed that newborns who had skin-to-skin contact with their fathers had less crying, an improved ability to soothe, and better prefeeding behavior.[1] Dads need the opportunity and scheduled time to interact with their babies. Fathers with little to no experience with babies before parenthood will have an expected learning curve; the learning process can be normalized with support from the other parent and extended family. With encouragement and increasing independence, dads' confidence is boosted and everyone wins.

---

1. Erlandsson K, Dsilna A, Fagerberg I, Christensson K. Skin-to-skin care with the father after cesarean birth and its effect on newborn crying and prefeeding behavior. *Birth*. 2007;34(2):105–114.

It bears addressing that moms and dads will have slightly different styles and techniques when handling their baby. As a pediatrician, I would gently advise all parents to not serve as a gatekeeper to their newborn son's care. There is more than one way to burp a baby, and there is more than one way to wipe a baby's bottom. All too often, one parent (I won't name names here) will decide there is a right way to burp the baby, or a proper way to put the new diaper on, and will habitually "correct" the other parent's methods. This undermines the other parent's skill building, as well as their confidence, and, ultimately, can serve as a roadblock for true baby-parent bonding. As a pediatrician wearing the hat of child health and safety, I would state that the first priority should be safety ("Safety first!" is a great motto for childhood in general). Infant safety means safe sleep practices (always laying an infant down on their back in a safe sleep environment, free from strangulation or suffocation hazards), crib safety (using a crib that meets current safety standards, with neither additional bedding nor crib bumpers), and car seat safety (appropriately fastening the infant into an infant car safety seat for all car rides), to name a few. If infant safety guidelines are being adhered to, it benefits infants and parents alike to avoid nit-picking specific nuances or methods. In general,

THE FAMILY JOURNEY

More Than One Route to the Same Destination

As parents of infants, our skills increase and we may have a "way" of doing things, whether feeding the baby, singing to them, or giving their evening bath. Just as our GPS suggests a few routes to our destination, we need to remember that there is more than one way to accomplish a task or goal. Assuming that safety and proper health guidelines are being followed, resist the temptation to constantly tweak or correct your partner's methods, as this may backfire into a *learned incompetence*. The corrected partner may feel that they're not good at certain tasks, and it can serve as a roadblock to their enthusiastic, invested participation. Be aware that gatekeeping of infant care chores may backfire and limit equity within your home.

dads can be more boisterous and may give more belly "zerberts" during diaper changes, for example; these differing parenting styles make for a more robust, varied, and stimulating environment in which your infant son will thrive.

Patterns are established in the early weeks and months of caring for an infant and running a household that will persist through the years. If chores and tasks are divided equitably between partners, this will continue for weeks, and before you can blink twice, the pattern is laid down for years to come. There is an oft-quoted saying in reference to raising young children: "The days are long, but the years are short."

THE FAMILY CALENDAR

It's not too soon to establish the concept of a family calendar. Technology, smartphone apps, and other types of shared calendars/to-do lists can really help in this realm. Your infant won't have soccer practice anytime soon, but a family calendar establishes a *trend* of teamwork from the beginning. One parent may take the lead in certain domains, while the other parent will take the lead in different domains, but *both* parents should be aware of the family schedule and household needs. One parent can be in charge of stocking up through warehouse diaper-purchasing trips, for example, but have a calendar alarm go off for that assigned parent once every couple of weeks. Personally, I'm old-school and, to this day, still use a large paper family calendar that we keep in the kitchen, but most parents' comfort zone is to use smartphone apps to stay organized. Most importantly, everyone should be logging on to the calendar and staying on top of the tasks. The point of emphasis here is that in female-male

Our Family Calendar

Sunday	Monday	Tuesday	Wednesday	Thursday	Friday	Saturday
	1 Tire appointment	2 Checkup at pediatrician 10:00 am	3 Grocery shopping	4 Warehouse shopping - Diapers - Toilet paper	5 Mowing The lawn	6 Ben's birthday party

partnerships in particular, the female parent isn't the gatekeeper of all family information. Both parents are adults and should team up. Invariably, real life has twists and turns: someone will get sick or have an important work project, and the other parent can step in and keep the ship afloat during that stretch. As time marches forward, the roles will reverse from time to time.

If your infant attends child care, important child care scheduling items should be included on the family calendar. Let child care staff know that when issues arise during your infant son's time at child care (eg, he comes down with a fever), staff can notify either or both parents, depending on the family plan and child care protocol. That includes dads. All too often,

THE FAMILY JOURNEY

Plot Your Way

The parent workload during a child's infancy includes the day-to-day feedings, diaper changes, laundry, and family meals. Don't forget about the bigger-picture chores that pile up as the mental load of parenthood.

Both parents should have regular discussions to ensure equity in big-picture chore planning and accomplishment as well. Here are some examples to continue your ongoing conversations with your partner.

- Arranging backup, evening, and weekend child care
- Stocking infant essentials in the home
- Washing and putting away the infant's laundry
- Scheduling pediatric/doctor appointments
- Administering vitamins/medicines
- Planning, packing, and unpacking for travel
- Organizing a weekly date night
- Being the family archivist (eg, saving photos, making albums, enlarging photos for display)
- Managing communication with child care providers, whether they provide care in your home or theirs or work at a child care center
- Arranging birthday, holiday, or special occasion gatherings, including day-of responsibilities

institutions' default setting is to call the mom, so make sure the prescribed child care phone-triage system for emergencies is laid out in a way that works for your family. Many schools and child care centers will explicitly ask families on sign-up and at regular intervals in what order they should make family notification phone calls for illness or unexpected emergencies. If there will be special child care classroom events (eg, Mother's or Father's Day programming—yes, even in infant child care!), make sure the staff knows to inform you with at least a week's (or more) notice so you can plan work accordingly.

HAVE A CONVERSATION

Dividing and Attending to Tasks

Is your son already 6 months old and you feel that some inequities in parenting and household tasks exist? Often mothers notice the mental load of parenthood; moms are well-known for keeping a mental list of both big- and small-picture tasks that need to get accomplished (eg, schedule the child's next health supervision visit with the pediatrician, buy more diapers, take the car to the shop for that weird braking sound). Your son's other parent may say "Just tell me what you need me to do," but this still puts the emphasis of the *remembering,* the mental load, on only one parent. It is helpful to divide big-picture to-dos, and the *remembering* to attend to these tasks, into themes to fall into one or the other parent's domain. Hold Sunday night meetings if needed to keep all caregivers on the same page, so all parties are aware of what is on deck for the upcoming week.

If as a parent, you feel you're well into the game but some unhealthy imbalances are occurring, it is time for honest conversation and reevaluation. Schedule this talk as you would any other appointment; it's important. A good time is after your infant is down for the evening because you'll want to discuss these issues as free of distractions as possible. It's also important to not talk about big-picture goal setting in the heat of the moment if an argument has started, because often, people are put on the defensive and both parties may say things in a more extreme manner than is intended or necessary, which will negatively affect the odds of a good, open discussion.

Finding the Right Time to Talk

Your son's infancy is a time of relative sleep deprivation, and none of us communicate properly when we are exhausted. When discussing any issue you have with your partner during your son's infancy, both parties should exhibit grace to not only each other but also themselves. Coming from a place of empathy and curiosity, the facts of how baby care and household tasks have progressed thus far can be stated. In any reevaluation, State of the Union–like conversation, "I feel" statements are helpful. Instead of being interpreted as an accusation of the other party, the information is being shared with vulnerability and a desire to come together. Inevitable road bumps will occur, and partners can come together to evaluate and troubleshoot solutions. It is with open, honest communication that parents can strategize ways to divide infant care and household tasks more equitably. An individual can determine only their own actions, however. If your partner is unwilling to have these teamwork discussions, professional guidance, whether through couples counseling or the advice of your health care professionals, may be needed.

THE FAMILY JOURNEY

Communication Toward a Better Path

Discussing hot-button issues in infant care with your partner can be a challenge. Put away screens and distractions and select a time when you're both relatively well rested. The inevitable trouble spots in your home equity should be discussed. "I feel" statements, rather than accusations, can help the conversation take a positive note, troubleshooting together as partners to achieve a shared goal of equity and role modeling for your son.

A template for this could look like this: *"I feel [identify the feeling] when [describe the issue]. I would like [propose a solution]."* These statements may alleviate feelings, but they don't change a partner's personality traits or temperaments, although a change in behavior is certainly possible over time for partners committed to each other, their son, and greater gender equity.

INVOLVEMENT OF FATHERS: FLIPPING THE SCRIPT ON THE IDEA OF A DEFAULT PARENT

The American Academy of Pediatrics journal *Pediatrics* published a 2016 clinical report, *Fathers' Roles in the Care and Development of Their Children,* that stated:

> The message [to support fathers' involvement] is clear: fathers do not parent like mothers, nor are they a replacement for mothers when they are not at home; they provide a unique, dynamic, and important contribution to their families and children. Parenting interventions to encourage father involvement seldom acknowledge fathers' coparenting role and need fundamental change.[2]

In our homes and within our own families, we can effect generational and societal change by recognizing the importance of the roles of moms *and* dads.

Benefits of Paternity Leave

When fathers take leave after the birth or adoption of a new baby, dads progress in their development as parents on a learning curve, confidence is gained, and the stage is set for years to come. Alexis Ohanian, the husband of Serena Williams and the cofounder of Reddit, wrote an essay for the *New York Times* in 2019 in which he candidly shares his experiences of how his paternity leave informed his relationship with his daughter. He shares:

> Spending a big chunk of time with Olympia when she was a newborn gave me confidence that I could figure this whole parenting thing out. As an only child with no cousins, I didn't grow up around babies; in fact, I had never held one until my daughter was born. At first, holding her terrified me. *I am a giant and she's so tiny… What if I break her?* I didn't—which was encouraging—and then I learned how to calm her crying, rock her to sleep and handle her toddler years with grace.[3]

---

2. Yogman M, Garfield CF; American Academy of Pediatrics Committee on Psychosocial Aspects of Child Health. Fathers' roles in the care and development of their children: the role of pediatricians. *Pediatrics.* 2016;138(1):e2016128.
3. Ohanian A. Parental leave was crucial after the birth of my child, and every father deserves it. *New York Times.* April 15, 2020. Accessed May 17, 2023. https://www.nytimes.com/2020/04/15/parenting/alexis-ohanian-paternity-leave.html.

Note that this is a family with access to much more help and financial resources than most of us. The benefits of paternity leave for *all* fathers and their burgeoning relationship with their babies, regardless of socioeconomic status, are evident.

The ability to take parental leave is a systemic issue, one we may not have a lot of individual control over. According to the US Department of Labor, "Paternity leave—and especially longer leaves of several weeks or months—can promote parent-child bonding, improve outcomes for children, and even increase gender equity at home and at the workplace."[4] Society has recognized the need for and noted the benefits of taking parental leave on the macro level; as families, we can take society further by making these life choices on the micro level. As parents, we can control only so much within our homes and workplaces, and major shifts still need to occur on systemic and national stages.

What Parents Should Know About Leave Options

The Family and Medical Leave Act (FMLA), passed into law in 1993, provides for job-protected, unpaid leave for eligible working parents, including same-sex parents. Under the FMLA, group health insurance coverage continues under the same terms and conditions as if the employee had not taken leave. Eligible parents can use up to 12 workweeks of leave in a 12-month period to care for a newborn or infant within 1 year after birth. The FMLA also allows for the placement of children who are adopted or part of the foster care system within 1 year of placement.[5] It is important to point out that because of eligibility requirements, the FMLA does not apply to about 40% of the workforce, and only 30% of organizations offer paid paternity leave, according to the Society for Human Resources Management.[6]

Parents in some parts of the country, in accordance with state and local ordinances, may also be eligible for partly paid parental leave and can take the remainder time as unpaid, job-protected leave. For example,

4. *Paternity Leave: Why Parental Leave for Fathers Is So Important for Working Families.* US Dept of Labor; 2016.
5. US Department of Labor. Fact sheet #28Q: taking leave from work for birth, placement, and bonding with a child under the FMLA. Accessed May 23, 2023. https://www.dol.gov/agencies/whd/fact-sheets/28q-taking-leave-for-birth-placement-child.
6. Levs J. One upside of COVID-19: kids are spending more time with dads. *Scientific American.* June 18, 2020. Accessed May 17, 2023. https://www.scientificamerican.com/article/one-upside-of-covid-19-kids-are-spending-more-time-with-dads.

California supports up to 8 weeks' paid leave in a rolling 12-week period, and San Francisco provides supplemental compensation.[7] At the time of this writing, more states and municipalities have started paid parental leave programs. Because of the lack of a federal, American paid parental leave policy, for many parts of the country, parental leave takes on a hodgepodge, patched-up quality, using a mix of saved PTO (paid time off) and vacation hours, supplemented with unpaid leave. Figuring out options is a difficult decision to balance family bonding with very real financial concerns.

Paternity leave in particular, and family leave in general, varies widely depending on where you live. Sweden is famous for extended paid family leave. Family leave is a win for gender equity. Studies show that if fathers spend even a short amount of time on parental leave, their long-term attitude toward domestic work is improved, resulting in more shared responsibilities in the long run.[8]

Many of the families I care for in my clinical pediatric practice take a rolling approach to parental leave. Dads and non-birthing parents can schedule some time off around the baby's birth and arrival home but then take the bulk of their time off when the mom or birthing parent has returned to work, giving the baby more continuous time overall with a parent on leave. For one of my patient's families, both parents are teachers. Their son was born in spring and the mom used her maternity leave.

THE FAMILY JOURNEY

Route Planning

Investigate parental leave options, for moms *and* dads. Think creatively and reach out to your networks to gain others' insight and brainstorm solutions toward greater equity in your son's care during infancy.

---

7. Stanford. Family care & parental bonding leave. Cardinal at Work. Accessed May 23, 2023. https://cardinalatwork.stanford.edu/benefits-rewards/time-away/leaves-of-absence/family-care-leave.
8. Gelin M. The pandemic has reshaped American fatherhood: can it last? *New York Times*. June 21, 2020. Accessed May 17, 2023. https://www.nytimes.com/2020/06/21/opinion/pandemic-fatherhood-fathers.html.

The family enjoyed the summer as family leave, and the father planned to use his "paternity leave" (in reality, PTO) in the fall to extend his time with his new son by another couple of months. His taking on a greater role in child care and running the household will hopefully set the stage for equitable teamwork as the years pass. Lead by example and model the future you want to see for your son.

ROLE MODELING AS PARENTS

Often gender equity, particularly in a female-male partnership, gets a bad rap: some say it's impossible to help genders become completely equal, that there are too many inherent differences, hormonal and otherwise. I would argue that equity is not all or nothing and that this isn't the time to throw up our hands, give up, and say "This is just how it is." Don't let perfection be the enemy of good. We should always be striving toward the goal of moving the needle toward a more equitable distribution of parenting and household tasks.

I envision my 3 sons, young adults in college at the time of this writing, in their futures: if they choose to begin a family with their partner, my hope for my sons is that they can live the full range of human experiences, including caregiving for their dependent(s). Men are benefitted when they can take part in such meaningful life experiences. Parents are wise to remember that gender equity doesn't benefit just women; it helps women *and* men live the full range of human experiences.

The global COVID-19 pandemic affected all aspects of our lives, most notably how our work and home lives intersect. Either through furloughs or work from home, almost overnight, a record number of fathers began navigating life as a stay-at-home parent or as a work-from-home parent. Although the global pandemic has been devastating for so many in health and economic security, the pandemic has also served as a pivot point for many families to more equitably shared parenting roles, even helping some families completely reevaluate their family choices moving forward. Because waves of SARS-CoV-2 variants affected where work is conducted and closed schools, families have been faced with reevaluating the division of child care and household labor among parents.

THE ROLE OF INFANT DEVELOPMENT IN PARENT INTERACTIONS

By the ages of 6 to 7 months, infants begin to develop the sense of *object permanence*. If you hide a toy under a blanket, an older infant will look for it. It is this developmental milestone that makes the game of peekaboo so fun; when you see a face momentarily disappear and then reappear, what could be more magical? Older infants are also becoming more aware of social dynamics and more discerning about familiar faces. Younger infants, 3 to 4 months of age, can usually be passed around at a family gathering, relative to relative, without any distress; try to do so with a 10-month-old and you'll observe a world of difference. Stranger anxiety, an aversion to new faces, emerges, and it is a typical stage of development for older infants.

THE FAMILY JOURNEY

Reading the Road Signs Along the Map's Route

Understanding your son's developmental stage and expected skills by age can help you learn how to bond and communicate with him more effectively. HealthyChildren.org, the official American Academy of Pediatrics website for parents, has resources on infants' and children's appropriate developmental stages. Both dads and moms should take a peek and should continue to learn about their son's developmental stages as time passes, to enhance their ability to bond with and support their son.

With these developments, older infants may also develop a "preference" for a particular parent and have a "mommy phase" or a "daddy phase" in which the infant seems to prefer one parent over the other. This is a typical, often brief developmental stage. Although for you as a parent the stage might cause anxiety, remember that this, too, shall pass. Continue one-on-one playtime with your son to encourage your bond.

Whether you and your partner are handling bath time, doing feeding time, or tucking your son in at night, the other parent might be reached for, but always continue to show your love. Recognize and normalize any feelings you may have of jealousy or inadequacy; doing so can be a challenge for a working parent, as we often internalize the preference of another parent as commentary on the fact that we work outside the home. It would be a mistake to simply give your son time with only the "preferred" parent, as this will only reinforce the trend. The pendulum will swing once again, and before then, you might even enjoy the periods when you are the "non-preferred" parent, but ensure equal time so any traditional caregiver gender lines are not reinforced.

TWO HOUSEHOLDS

American families are diverse in their structures, members, and living arrangements, and the American Academy of Pediatrics recognizes that we do not all fit the 2-parent household stereotype. How can dads not living in the same home as their newborn or infant get better involved during their son's first year after birth? The benefits for kids to have fathers' involvement has been backed by research. The US Department of Health and Human Services has reported that "fathers who are involved, nurturing, and playful with their infants have children with higher IQs, as well as better linguistic and cognitive capacities."[9] Active communication, schedule setting, and cooperation between both partners are key to achieving infant time with both parents. The days and weeks get busy and then fly by, so my recommendation is, if possible, to have a routine schedule in place, with a healthful dose of flexibility for when life, illness, and other unforeseen circumstances arise.

If a father does not express interest in being part of an infant son's life, this is something to be explored, with family counseling being a good option to troubleshoot solutions and learn coping strategies. A key aspect of caregiving is that the grown-ups in a baby's immediate circle are invested in emotional connection and the bettering of their parenting skills as the baby grows. A family may need to make some difficult choices if one parent is unprepared for the humbling and rewarding investment

---

9. Rosenberg J, Wilcox WB. *The Importance of Fathers in the Healthy Development of Children.* US Dept of Health and Human Services; 2006. Accessed May 23, 2023. https://www.childwelfare.gov/pubpdfs/fatherhood.pdf.

THE FAMILY JOURNEY

Multiple Routes

The American Academy of Pediatrics recognizes the diversity among families raising infants and young children in the United States. Two-parent households have different needs than separate households, which are distinct from single-parent households. Those of us who are working single parents are leading by example and modeling for our sons that people across genders, whether woman, man, or person (nonbinary, gender fluid, gender nonconforming, or more), are strong and powerful.

of being an involved caregiver in a child's life, and they may need to be open to reevaluation as time goes on.

I mentioned *strategic* (or *weaponized* or *feigned*) *incompetence* in Chapter 2, Nurturing Our Sons to Be Better Men, Even Before They Are Born. Continue to be aware of this phenomenon because patterns for household chores in your son's infancy will tend to stick over time. If one partner feels weak in a skill set required for a particular task, don't passive-aggressively sabotage the job; *talk* about it. Exchange that task for another task; don't simply dump it onto the pile of responsibilities of the default parent.

Not good at laundry? It's not enough to botch a load and then be "excused" from that task moving forward. Assume responsibility for other home maintenance projects, outdoor jobs, or not only being in charge of scheduling your infant son's pediatric appointments but also taking him to the appointments. The dangerous aspect of strategic incompetence is that it may give the partner with an offense a pass moving forward, as if there is no expectation of the need for their participation in the realm of household chores. This is a mistake and it's important to set the stage in your son's infancy for years to come. Be aware of this phenomenon and call it out when it becomes a pattern.

WORDS MATTER: PHRASES AT STAGES THAT DO US NO FAVORS

Language matters, and words matter. When a dad changes his infant's diaper, he's being a parent, not "Mr Mom." When a father feeds his baby a bottle of expressed breast milk, he's not performing "mom duties," he is parenting his infant. As a family and as partners raising an infant son, ensure that your words represent your larger parenting goals. Dads aren't "helping" or "babysitting"; they are parenting.

The words we use with each other matter, and the words we use with our infants help them developmentally for a lifetime. Words and robust communication are vital to an infant's early brain development. Going into your infant's room in the morning and greeting them with a soft "Good morning" starts to have meaning to them. When you say your child's name to them aloud, they begin to understand that it's their name. Dads' words specifically will help our sons' brain development and boost their communication skills for years to come.

THE FAMILY JOURNEY

Read the Signage Along Your Route

The words we use with each other, and the words we use with our infant sons, matter. Spoken/signed words *and* written words matter; it's not too early to introduce your son to the written word via board books. I always suggest to the families I care for in my clinical pediatrics practice to keep board books available in every part of the home, not only to make impromptu reading sessions more convenient but also to allow older babies to explore the pages themselves (Yes, chewing on a board book page counts!). During infancy, enjoy and explore all subject matter. To expand your reading list, subsequent chapters include age-appropriate reading suggestions that are specific to gender-equity issues.

INTERACTIONS WITH EXTENDED FAMILY OR THE GREATER COMMUNITY

Parenthood comes with many lessons and life experiences, a significant one being that you will fully learn that well-intentioned people, including loved ones, can make spontaneous statements without considering the full implications of their words. We are all human after all, and often, thoughts jump out of our mouths before being filtered by our brain (I, certainly, am quite seasoned at this phenomenon). How many times have we bumped into a father doing grocery shopping with kids in tow and thought to ourselves "Great job! What a great dad!" Certainly, great parenting in all forms should be applauded, but unless we're also complimenting every mom we bump into in the same store, our underlying biases, whether we are female, male, or another gender, are revealing themselves. Underlying biases are the mental pictures we hold about people, in this case, about what makes a man, a man (and what makes a woman, a woman). We aren't necessarily aware of our biases because we've learned them over time from our culture, upbringing, and personal experiences.

Similarly, when grandparents, extended family, or friends visit and your infant son spits up, requiring a wardrobe change, or needs a fresh diaper, there's a temptation, if the father is the parent to respond to this immediate parenting obligation, to stand and cheer. Again, unless the mother is also being applauded on the regular, this reveals our inner gender biases and we are wise to become aware of them and work toward modification. I always joke in my clinic that we parents don't get report cards to evaluate how "well" we are doing at this parenting thing, so I'm personally in favor of us standing and cheering for dads *and* moms performing daily caregiving tasks.

THE FAMILY JOURNEY

Post Signs That Reflect Your Gender-Equity Goals

Perception becomes reality. Ensure that if you choose home decor or infant clothing with writing on it, the message supports your greater gender-equity goals.

THE FAMILY JOURNEY

Responding to a Backseat Driver Like a Pro

How do we handle grandparents effusively or disproportionately complimenting the father for performing basic parenting chores? Over the years, I've become a fan of smiling and nodding while speaking my truth. For example, you can redirect the statement with a smile and an even tone of voice: "Yes, Ethan is great at changing diapers; we've learned that prevention is key to prevent painful diaper rashes." Keep your responses direct and simple. Depending on your relationship with these relatives, you can even gently point out the greater ramifications of such statements as related to gender roles.

Gender equity is partly about appearance, and as silly or superficial as it may seem, the manner in which you dress your infant can actually make an impact. Visual appearances can sway how we as parents and our family and friends view our sons. Certain color schemes are fine (eg, sticking with shades of blue, which is a beautiful color!), but graphic tees are also popular and can share phrases that might not be consistent with your greater gender-equity goals. Similar to the theme of the Words Matter section earlier in this chapter, if you're gifted a graphic tee with "Boys will be boys" emblazoned on the front, I'd be cautious about your son wearing an item that perpetuates a negative stereotype. A "Boys will be boys" onesie might actually make for a great spit-up cloth that doesn't leave the home (insert a wink emoji here).

YOUR SON'S INFANCY: ESTABLISHING HEALTHY PATTERNS EARLY

At the time of this writing, the 2-month-old son of one of the lovely families I care for in my clinic was due for his routine health supervision visit with necessary vaccinations. This is their first child, and Dad brought him in for the visit. This father was confident, came prepared with all the baby's needed gear, had a great list of questions saved to his smartphone (with contributions from the baby's mom), and tended to his son's needs expertly and efficiently, including freshening his diaper and soothing him after the vaccines were administered. Happily, I see a fantastic proportion of my patients' fathers bringing them into my clinic, for both health checkups and focused or sick visits.

It is important for kids to know they can count on dads in times of sickness and in times of health. Much like emperor penguin fathers can protect their unhatched chick eggs, human fathers can provide safety and security to their babies. When fathers, particularly those in female-male partnerships, are involved in their infant son's daily routines, everyone wins: an infant's development is boosted; fathers live the full range of human experiences, including parenthood; mothers' unpaid labors are better balanced; and the needle is moved toward greater gender equity. The stage is set in infancy for a boy's childhood that normalizes equitable parenting. These critical early months of infancy may or may not be how we were raised ourselves, but we have a responsibility to establish these patterns to break free of the chains of generational inequities. Our sons, our dads, and our society deserve it.

Blink twice and your infant son will celebrate his first birthday, and once again, you will pivot to meet the challenge of raising a self-aware, energetic, loving young boy through the toddler and preschool ages. Communicating and role modeling for your son is of vital importance to set the stage to meet your big-picture goals of a whole-person boy with an equitable view of genders in our world.

RECOMMENDED RESOURCE FOR PARENTS AT THIS STAGE

Mangino K. *Equal Partners: Improving Gender Equality at Home.* St Martin's Press; 2022. Tackling household gender-inequality problems, Mangino discusses how cultural norms and traditions influence gender behavior as much as structural laws and policies.

Chapter 4

Nurturing Toddlers and Preschoolers to Be Better Men: Shaping Our Sons' Worldview

My mother-in-law loves to lecture me on the state of my house as if I don't live with someone that she raised."[1] I read this biting commentary online recently. There are many layers and questions to unpack within the statement. There are so many layers that I'm reminded of a Russian matryoshka nesting doll; the largest doll is opened to reveal yet more dolls residing within.

Included in the layered questions: Why is the state of the home the responsibility of the female partner? Why, generationally, is this mother-in-law seemingly not even aware that she is perpetuating the patriarchal idea that in a female-male partnership, it is the female partner's "responsibility" to ensure a tidy home, through her commentary? Why didn't she and any partner of hers raise their own son to have a stake in shared ownership over the state of a shared living space? Understandably, generational ideas about male and female roles within the home, gendered roles, are so embedded within our culture that we can barely recognize them for what they are. And sadly, women are often the individuals perpetuating these patriarchal philosophies without even realizing so. We need to be self-aware and we can certainly do better.

---

1. @oneawkwardmom. My mother-in-law loves to lecture me on the state of my house as if I don't live with someone that she raised. February 21, 2022. Accessed May 17, 2023. https://twitter.com/oneawkwardmom/status/1495818999422234630.

THE NEED TO CHANGE THE GENDERED NARRATIVE

Introducing Chores

Kids do as they see. We as parents need to change the gendered narrative. Our toddler and preschool sons need to *see* male parents engaged in the equitable running of a household. They need to see dads vacuuming the living room, they need to see dads cooking dinner, and they need to join fathers to buy food at the grocery store. Boys at 2, 3, and 4 years of age are also old enough and developmentally capable to participate in simple yet meaningful tasks to care for the shared space of a home, setting the stage for their participation for years to come. Young boys can and should carry lightweight bags into the house from the grocery store (Just be careful of the eggs!).

Let me share a story for the purpose of making a point about raising toddler boys. In my pediatric office, during the summer checkup season, I often ask my junior high and high school patients "What are your chores at home?" One day, teenaged boy siblings and their parent literally laughed out loud when I asked them this question. I then pulled out an old-school paper prescription pad (we've used electronic prescriptions for years) and wrote each boy a "prescription" to be tasked with more household responsibilities. I wanted the family to have a physical, tangible reminder of my recommendation. That's because the boys were in my office with their mom, who agreed that the boys should tackle more chores, yet apparently, the boys' father, who was not present that day, felt it would simply be "quicker and easier" to perform the tasks himself than to engage in a power struggle with his sons. This dad would rather avoid confrontation than implement daily patterns that would set the stage for years, and generations, to come. This conflict avoidance doesn't help anyone, most of all the boys themselves, as they need these life skills to be functional roommates and space sharers in the future.

Why am I talking about teenagers in a chapter about toddlers? Toddlers *love* to imitate the grown-ups around them. *Now* is the ideal time to capitalize on this important developmental milestone. There is a cliché that tweens and teens will groan and resist chores (I continue to debunk this myth for chapters to come). If you wait until your son is 12 years old to introduce the idea of contributing to the shared workload of running a household, you've waited too long. The timeliness of introducing the concept of working together to care for the family's shared space is developmentally perfect for 2-, 3-, and 4-year-olds. Toddlers always watch the grown-ups around them and use their observations to inform their pretend play. Have you watched a 1-year-old with a smartphone? They see the adults on phones and love to emulate us. Give a 2-year-old a duster, or teach them to place wet towels into the dryer, and you have a kid puffed up with pride, their confidence boosted, and another family member actively helping around the home.

The evening after I saw the 2 teen patients for whom I wrote paper prescriptions for chores, I wrote on my personal social media page, encouraging others to nurture the chores as the norm with their children. I wrote, "Start early, friends. Kids won't magically want to scrub toilets at the age of 12!" Nurturing toddlers' and preschoolers' natural, helpful instincts, and establishing patterns early, creates a foundation on which to build for years to come.

Kids rise to expectations, and perception becomes reality. Toddlers are energetic, curious explorers. If toddler boys' natural tendencies are labeled as "wild and uncontrollable," you'll unconsciously perpetuate a pattern. If we approach each of our son's ages as growth and learning opportunities, we can flip the script and nurture our young sons to exhibit *all* human characteristics. Yes, this includes energy, mood swings, and power struggles as toddlers realize they're independent from their parents, but it also includes empathy and a huge ability to love and care for others.

Navigating the Comments

My 3 sons were all born within the span of 18 months, so I've navigated the world for years with boys who resemble triplets instead of twins close in age to their older brother. At the grocery store, on vacations, in restaurants, you name it, the world told me "You must have your hands full" and would typically assume that my boys, all boys, were wild, uncontrollable, and chaotic. I tried to be mindful of these interactions with strangers and consider them from the perspective of my young sons. Our children are always listening to us, and they're always watching us. I usually responded to inquisitive, random people commenting on my brood of sons with some version of "They're great kids and I'm lucky to have them." Honestly, I wasn't speaking to the stranger in these moments. I wanted my sons to hear how much I loved them and how wanted they were. Overheard praise speaks powerfully to a child's self-esteem. Let your kids hear you praise them, not just to them but to others. If a child has a strong sense of self and self-esteem, this acts as a buffer, a force field, that will serve them for years to come. They'll feel empowered to be themselves, whatever that looks like; they'll be bully proofed; and they'll know how to make others in their world feel loved and cared for.

You know the phrase "speak it into existence"? Many believe that our thoughts and mindset determine our outcomes. Some call this *manifest destiny.* Speak your goals into existence, and assume the best for your young sons as they grow. Yes, I am an optimist, and I strongly believe that you'll get what you think you're going to get. Let's together debunk myths about young boys and expand our notions of what a young boy *can* be.

DAILY INTERACTIONS PROVIDE COMMUNICATION OPPORTUNITIES

From a developmental standpoint, during the ages of 2, 3, and 4 years, toddlers and preschoolers are learning valuable communication skills. Toddlers' *receptive* language skills (what they're able to understand) emerge well before their *expressive* language skills (what they're able to verbally express back to us). This finding is consistent with one of my mottos I believe most about our kids: "Children understand so much more than we adults often give them credit for." In the case of toddlers, this is literally true because your 2-year-old son is absorbing messaging in amounts that far exceed his ability to articulate the message back to you.

What this means from a practical standpoint during the chaos of keeping tiny humans alive is that we'll want to realize that our sons are watching us, listening to us, and learning by our example daily. A child's life from their birth to the age of 5 years shapes their self-esteem and identity for the rest of their life, and the messaging and communicating we share with our sons during this critical period will influence our boys for years to come. Yes, there will be days that we are simply in survival mode, trying to make it to bedtime with everyone alive and the home *relatively* intact. That said, we parents need to remember the powerful impact we make on our boys, whether we are conscious of it in each moment or not.

It's so important to *communicate* with our toddler and preschool boys. When our sons are toddlers, communication means turning off screens, narrating our daily lives together, and reading board books together. My favorite analogy is that of a television cooking-show host who talks us through recipes during the cooking process. In a similar fashion, narrate life as you add ingredients and seasoning, adjust the heat, talk through the process… That's what we should do with our young kids, even though at times we may feel a bit silly. The goal is to surround your child with words. As your son grows, your communication together will evolve and become more robust.

THE FAMILY JOURNEY

Reading Road Signs

Communication means more than talking *to* our sons; we also need to give our boys space to communicate their feelings back to us. Listening, and pausing, matters. Often, we grown-ups pipe up to fill empty spaces; even when our sons are young, we should practice simply being present for our sons, so they can feel seen and heard by us. When we do this, we not only understand our boys better but also model for our sons important life skills they'll use themselves.

Communication means so much more than the mere exchange of information. The back-and-forth, the listening, the reading of expressions, and the reading of emotions. Recognizing mood and attitude, and the simple act of creating space for the other person to express their feelings and opinions, is so important in the development of a child's self-esteem and self-worth. There's an often-used expression that is attributed to Catherine Wallace: "Listen earnestly to anything [your children] want to tell you, no matter what. If you don't listen eagerly to the little stuff when they are little, they won't tell you the big stuff when they are big, because to them all of it has always been big stuff."[2]

Although much of the toddler stage of parenting focuses on discipline, remember that the most important way to help shape your son's behavior

---

2. Goodreads. Accessed May 17, 2023. https://www.goodreads.com/quotes/241128-listen-earnestly-to-anything-your-children-want-to-tell-you.

is with positive reinforcement and time-in, as opposed to time-outs. Having pleasant, positive one-on-one time with your child is 80% of the job. Whether performing daily necessary tasks such as the nighttime bath or taking a neighborhood family walk together, this positive family time together goes a long way in supporting your young son to feel that he has been heard and to know that he matters.

Many families use the game of "apples and onions" or "highs and lows" at mealtimes or during the bedtime routine to foster better communication. Take turns with your son sharing the best (apples) and not-so-great (onions) parts of the day. This works at *all* ages. When you pick up your boy from preschool, asking "How was your day?" may or may not get a vibrant response. If you dig a little deeper, you'll learn about the scenarios and daily events that matter to your kid. Taking turns with these simple questions between parent and son helps nurture empathy in your son, as he can learn about *your* day. Showing our kids that we as adults also have trials and tribulations, by sharing about our day in simple terms they will understand, not only normalizes the struggles of life but provides a great way for your son to work those empathy muscles.

Beyond communication, make it a routine to recognize and celebrate all genders in your home. Recently, I had an 18-month-old patient in for his routine health supervision visit. His parents brought board books to entertain him while waiting to see me. I love this approach for many reasons: one of the best things parents can do to boost literacy and strengthen future academic success is to provide their child with early and frequent exposure to books. Also, you never know whether your child's pediatrician will have an emergency or situation causing your family to wait longer than expected. My patient's favorite book was a Wonder Woman board book, and he was matter-of-factly checking it out as I walked into his examination room. No pomp and circumstance needed, as this family simply chose to show their son a variety of gender images, modeling positive female role models, including superheroes, in their day-to-day lives. The simple day-to-day choices are the most powerful.

As kids grow, they explore and experiment with different personas and identities. Consider any 4-year-old child having a field day in the dress-up corner of their preschool classroom. As kids grow and learn more about themselves and how they fit into the world around them, it's developmentally appropriate for them to "try on" different alter egos, including gender-diverse ideas. Has your 3-year-old son tried on a princess costume? He is curious;

it's no big deal. Know that your son will experiment with different realities during this process, and remind your partner and others in your son's world that this is a developmentally appropriate, typical stage. We parents are wise to play it cool, accept and love our sons, and not sweat the small stuff.

A family I spoke with talked about how their toddler son adored his older sister. He went through a prolonged phase during which he wore a hand-me-down nightgown from his sister around the house, for "about 6 months." His parents didn't overthink it, didn't swoop in and "correct" their son, and, frankly, realized that this particular nightgown was pretty darn comfortable (smart kid!). Time passed and the stage passed; their son outgrew this preference on his own. This mom and dad were conscious and careful to neither shame their boy nor judge him, were not making unnecessary commentary, and were not creating issues where there were none. Realize that your son's development is a fluid situation that will go through stages and experimentation.

Let your young son see, and bear witness, that either parent can handle everything. A smart mom I interviewed alternates weekday "morning duty" caring for her 2-year-old son with her male partner. Using this method, Mom can reliably go to the gym in the morning before work. Just as important as seeing his mom care for herself and her mental and physical health, the 2-year-old boy also sees that his dad can and will be able to handle the weekday morning routine of getting the family up and out the door. Parents who communicate with each other to strategize how to best divide child care and household duties serve as an example for their child as they grow older.

THE FAMILY JOURNEY

Ensuring the Correct Gear for the Road

Whether toys or board books, surround your son with a variety of influences that are either gender neutral or show an alternative to older notions of occupations and hobbies. Books about female superheroes and nurturing males, and gender-neutral toys such as building blocks, send a broader message to young boys about our roles in society.

Swiss psychologist Jean Piaget has famously said that "play is the work of childhood." Varied books and toys will help shape your son's early worldview. A few families I spoke with use gender-neutral play kits with age-specific toys, tailored to their son's developmental phase. When my boys were young, I let my friends know I was in the market for a previously owned play kitchen (I had sticker shock from looking at new options, and I knew my sons would love it regardless of whether it came from a new package or was already built—already built, frankly, being a bonus). One day, a trusted friend called from a garage sale (this was before the ubiquitous nature of texting; I know, I'm showing my age here)—we hit the jackpot, because a beautiful, already-assembled play kitchen was for sale at a fraction of the price of new. Did I care that the color scheme was mainly white with lots of pink accents? Pink cabinets, pink handles on all the knobs, and a pink faucet? Heck, I don't like the color pink. But this kitchen? SOLD to the happy family with 3 little boys. We loved this kitchen greatly, and I was pretty wistful when it was time to finally pass it on to a different family when my kids, years later, outgrew imaginative play. Sidenote: The best kitchen "supplies" are actual, real food containers, such as yogurt containers, empty cardboard boxes, and used egg cartons, cleaned out and repurposed as toys; they are realistic and green because such repurposing keeps the items out of landfills for the moment.

There are no "boy colors" or "girl colors." My wise friend has said "Colors are for everyone!" and I think this is a wonderful phrase to say repeatedly in the presence of our young kids to swim against the tide. A family I spoke with told me that after getting a haircut, their son selected a pink balloon at the salon and the stylist asked the parent "Is that OK?" This mom said "It's a balloon! It doesn't even matter because he's only 3. It's a balloon and it's a color. Do some parents actually say no?" The sad truth is that some parents would actually say no. Don't limit your son's options; let him explore and try out different styles and personas.

A family I spoke with shared a story about going to a shoe store. Their preschool daughter loved the color yellow; it was her favorite color at the time. No less than 2 or 3 employees felt the need to tell her mother "We only have boy shoes in yellow." Mom matter-of-factly asked that they bring those out and her daughter was elated to leave the store in her brand-new yellow shoes. Similarly, your son may have a particular favorite color. Young kids' shoes and clothes are so well loved before being quickly outgrown, so I empower you to go for this pair of shoes and realize that it will send a great message of support and love to your child (and will be outgrown in just a couple of months).

Dolls are for everyone. Young boys love to demonstrate care and empathy to dolls. Your son watches you care for him, so of course he wants to emulate you and, in turn, care for his own "child." Don't overthink this, and normalize young boys playing with dolls. Be prepared for relatives, especially grandparents, to comment on the doll (or not, as maybe you are lucky). Just as playing dress-up allows young children to experiment with different identities and personas, playing in a play kitchen or caring for a doll allows boys to explore what it means to practice the life skill of providing sustenance, or caring for another human.

THE FAMILY JOURNEY

The Scenic Route

It's typical and healthy for kids to go through phases. Don't overthink a phase if your son is exploring different identities. Just as a 4-year-old will try on every outfit at the preschool dress-up corner, both firefighter and princess, experimentation is part of how a child learns how they fit into the world.

Consider how you spend your time and what that means for the examples and narratives you provide for your son. A family I spoke with always shares the seasonal park district guide with their kids when it arrives in the mail, looking over the options with their children. When they discuss different options for their kids, they work to be self-aware and to prevent preconceived notions of what their girls and their boys may be interested in or want to learn more about. They intentionally ask both their boys and their girls whether they're interested in T-ball or ballet, wanting all their kids to be open to the spectrum of possibilities available to them. All too often, even at this young age, we define for boys and girls that "boys do *this*, and girls do *that*." Everyone wins if we leave as many doors open as possible.

One of my patients' parents, a parent of 2 young boys and no girls, shared with me that they have family friends with daughters who will "sit for hours crafting," which is great, but the friends would preemptively tell this mom of young boys "Oh, but you have boys, so they won't do that," which is not so great. Who are we to preemptively decide what our sons will and won't enjoy doing? I wonder how many young boys aren't even offered certain activities to try in the first place because the grown-ups around them assume they won't be interested. Or if the activity opportunity presents itself, the grown-ups make comments or voice opinions that shut the activity down prematurely. Self-awareness is key here.

EMOTIONAL LITERACY

As a pediatrician, I think about child developmental ages and stages as a toddler/preschooler grows into a grade schooler, and then a middle schooler, to eventually become a young man. What are the steps we should think about in these early days to ensure we are supporting an emotionally healthy individual with good communication skills and appropriate outlets for their passions?

Narrow expectations of what boys can be and do, even as toddlers and preschoolers, puts boys into a box, which can chip away at their self-esteem and lead to pent-up issues manifesting later in their lives. Glennon Doyle writes about the narrow expectations for our sons in her book *Untamed:*

> Our men are caged.... The parts of themselves they must hide to fit into those cages are the slices of their humanity that our culture has labeled "feminine"—traits like mercy, tenderness, softness, quietness, kindness, humility, uncertainty, empathy, connection. We tell them, "Don't be these things because these are feminine things to be. Be anything but feminine." The problem is that the parts of themselves that our boys have been banished from are not feminine traits; they are human traits.... Human qualities are not gendered.[3]

Three-year-old boys can be rambunctious, and they can be loving. We grown-ups should nurture all these diverse aspects of our boys' identity.

---

3. Doyle G. *Untamed.* Dial Press; 2020.

As a pediatrician, I often discuss with my patients' families that an important developmental stage of the toddler years is when the toddler is realizing they are their own person, separate from their parents. Infants have such a strong connection to parents that they don't quite realize they are an individual. It can be somewhat scary and jarring to realize you're having your own emotions; for a toddler, the very human experience of becoming angry or frustrated is magnified because the toddler is realizing how scary it is to even have this emotion, compounding the drama. Much of emotionally healthy parenting in the toddler stage is helping your son identify the feelings he's having. Try "I understand you're having fun at the park, but it's now time to get into the car to get home for dinner. You might feel frustrated about it, but we still need to leave." Identify the feeling and put words to it, modeling for your son how to healthfully identify and express the feelings.

THE FAMILY JOURNEY

Roadblocks

It is developmentally appropriate for toddlers to realize they are an individual. Couple this with your son's still-growing language skills, and inevitably, power struggles will happen. When possible, present your son with acceptable choices and lean into positive reinforcement as a main discipline strategy. Consult your son's pediatrician for advice specific to your situation, if needed. *Discipline* doesn't mean "punishment"; it means "to teach," to guide your son toward an acceptable framework of behavior. These baby steps are an important part of the journey to nurture our boys to be better men.

A family I spoke with talked about the importance of identifying feelings. This family makes a point to collect specific board books on the subject of feelings to help their son identify how he is feeling. These parents agree that even during a tantrum or meltdown, they will work to name the feeling while still establishing boundaries. For example, they will say "I know you're feeling mad that we need to leave. It's OK to feel mad. But we don't hit other people."

To raise *whole* boys means to raise emotionally literate boys who are aware of their feelings and the feelings of others. Toddlers can learn the building blocks of emotional literacy with their parents daily to set the stage for years to come.

In addition to helping our young sons identify their feelings, we need to teach our boys that it's OK to ask others for help. In a discussion with Elissa Strauss for CNN Health, Don McPherson, who coined the phrase "aspirational masculinity" (a counterpoint to toxic masculinity; more on this in Chapter 7, Nurturing High School Boys to Be Better Men), says regarding boys asking for help, "I truly believe this, and I am saying this to you as someone who doesn't know how to do this, . . . [n]ot asking for help is what keeps boys confined in the narrowness of masculinity and leads us to suicide, violence, abusive relationships and abusive relationships with ourselves." Strauss continues, "Asking for help creates space in which boys can see their needs and vulnerabilities as something that can and should be addressed. Doing so will help them move beyond the narrow definition of masculinity and be their full, complex selves, whatever that may be."[4]

So what does this mean? When your 4-year-old son is timid on the playground and he wants you to hold his hand as he walks a balance beam, or when your 3-year-old is struggling to put away his wooden board puzzle, don't overthink things, and certainly don't derisively tell your son to "Man up" and figure it out on his own. Even in these seemingly minor circumstances that you think will be forgotten, your son will remember the space that was created for him to ask for help. Normalize the give-and-take of asking for and receiving help. In this, be sure to ask your toddler son for help, such as help setting the table with unbreakable dinnerware, help bringing the lightweight groceries into the house, or help caring for the new baby sibling. This help should be a two-way street. And the help of parents working together models this further for our sons. Community begins at home within our families.

---

4. Strauss E. Talking to boys about being a boy. CNN Health. June 10, 2022. Accessed May 17, 2023. https://www.cnn.com/2022/06/10/health/masculinity-conversation-boys-wellness/index.html.

THE FAMILY CALENDAR

All too often, the female parent in a female-male partnership becomes the gatekeeper of family logistics, appointments, and information. This is often cited as the "mental load" of motherhood. Make sure you have an egalitarian system to keep track of family logistics, including specifics such as pediatric and dental appointments, school functions, and shopping lists for necessary household items, so *both* parents have access.

I prefer a large paper calendar in the kitchen, but I'm showing my age here (although paper doesn't crash the way technology can). Many parents prefer a shared calendar app to keep everyone on the same page; an additional benefit is that it's portable in your smartphone, so if you happen to stop for groceries on the way home from work, you've got your list with you. It is of vital importance that the gatekeeping of family and household logistics does not fall to only a single parent, and it doesn't matter who works inside or outside the home or whose labor is paid or unpaid. We're all adults, so any parent can and should be able to navigate the tasks of running a household, including daily logistics and special events.

Along these lines, if the mom has to travel for work or has to attend to other situations that will keep her from the family temporarily, the dad should already be so well versed in family routines to easily have the skills to keep the ship afloat. Routinely on social media, you'll observe viral posts about comically detailed instructions for a dad while the mom is away for 48 hours (or less); these posts make me sad. A dad isn't a "babysitter";

Our Family Calendar

Sunday	Monday	Tuesday	Wednesday	Thursday	Friday	Saturday
10	11	12	13	14	15	16
	Swim lesson noon	Make cookies for bake sale	Gymnastics 2:00 pm	Grocery shopping	HVAC inspection	Spread mulch

THE FAMILY JOURNEY

Consult the Road Map

The family calendar will continue to be an important tool for shared teamwork in running a household. Knowing what is happening when, knowing which grocery and bulk items are needed at which intervals, and planning for future events, travel, and holidays should all be included on the calendar. Partners should evaluate their system to ensure that one parent is not being overburdened with a disproportionate amount of the "mental load" of parenthood.

he's a *parent* and he'll figure it out. When *your* son is an adult, is this the scenario you envision for him, should he choose to become a parent? Or perhaps you hope he'll do better?

A dad's system and methods may not be the exact same as the mom's, but as long as everyone is alive, fed, and safe, the details don't particularly matter. Different parenting styles can be an advantage. I wouldn't have video footage of my young sons bouncing onto and off of couches in sync with the beat of the Ramones' "Blitzkreig Bop" if they weren't under the care of their capable father while I was out. My sons were safe, and they had a blast engaging in activities that their mom had certainly never even thought of.

THE FAMILY JOURNEY

Investing in the Road

The toddler years are a great opportunity to get your kids into the habit of contributing to the household. Toddlers by definition are eager to please and love to emulate the grown-ups around them. Take advantage of this developmental phase. Even when he's at a young age, involve your son in the running of the household. It may seem like more work in the early stages, but it will pay dividends in the long run.

Some families perpetuate an outdated tradition of women being the only members of the family to arrange holiday gatherings, birthdays, and family get-togethers. The invite list, which food will be served and activities will occur, the preparations before and cleanup after—who is managing these details? Many times, gendered patterns are so ingrained in our families and in society that we don't even think twice about the fact that women are literally running the show. Be aware of this trend, and swim against the tide.

A natural way for families to divide the mental load and plan for special holidays and gatherings is that dads coordinate with their partner and side of the family and moms coordinate with their partner and side of the family. This seems like common sense, but unfortunately, common sense isn't all that common. I've been shocked over the years by how it seemed to be an unspoken rule that I, the female parent, was in charge of who/what/when/ where when it came to visits with my kids' dad's enormous family. Even after the divorce was finalized, I learned of female relatives from my kids' dad's side of the family wanting my permission for the kids to attend an event on that side of the family. Perhaps their dad can coordinate this? Yet this happens in many families, every day, including from female relatives. Understandably, it may be gendered generational trends at play. Be aware of it, call it out (or "call it in") when you encounter it, and establish new trends and boundaries. Identifying and calling out (or calling in) these situations and creating a new normal is the only way we can stem the tide of women being solely responsible for the mental load of parenthood.

THE FAMILY JOURNEY

Putting the Brakes On

A **call in** is a gentler version of **a callout,** in which you challenge someone directly, possibly among others, about bad behaviors. A call in is a supportive communication between the 2 involved parties, with a gentle question such as "Please explain what you mean by that, because I have a different perspective." A call in, while still calling for change, is asking the other person to bring empathy and patience to the table. Calling in treats the other person as a peer, someone with whom you still want to keep a healthy relationship.

So for the next family event, parents should ask themselves "Who is doing the meal planning and cooking? Who is serving the food? Who is cleaning up the kitchen and dishes after?" Parents should have a conversation and model for their son what they want the future to look like. Female family running the holiday show means boys witness only women planning and orchestrating these events, so their expectation when they are adults with their own families may be exactly what they witnessed while growing up.

CHILD CARE CENTER/ PRESCHOOL LOGISTICS

Both parents should have clear lines of communication with child care and school staff. Even in this day and age, I've been surprised over the years by how school staff often defaults to the old-school notion of calling *moms* when the kid has an issue in school. Organized child care centers and schools will have a delineated phone tree with an order of numbers to call if (really, when) your child has an issue in school, whether it's coming down with a fever, vomiting, or facing another scenario in which they need to be picked up early. There is also likely a chain of command for feedback on classroom dynamics, any social issues that come up within the classroom. Ensure that your son's school staff knows to call either or both parents with issues, and remember that dads can be ranked first on the phone tree, particularly important if the dad is a stay-at-home parent.

If you find that only you as a mom are getting well-intentioned emails about classroom dynamic issues (eg, bullying in prekindergarten), when you respond, make sure you cc the dad on the reply, and begin your email by asking school staff to please keep him in the loop. If we are not consciously swimming against the tide, the default setting always seems to be to place moms as the gatekeeper of logistics and situations, and this will only serve to perpetuate decades of patriarchal trends.

Your toddler or preschooler will have special, fun events at their child care center or preschool, including days such as Halloween costume parades, Mother's and Father's Day programming, and more. Keep an open line of communication with your child's school staff to make sure you have at least 1 to 2 weeks' notice before special events so you can arrange work logistics (or have another trusted adult, such as a grandparent, attend in your place). As my 4 kids grew through these ages, I was surprised at the number of "Come visit your kid in school for a poetry tea!" events given

THE FAMILY JOURNEY

Involving Others to Help You Reach Your Destination

Well-intentioned school staff may default to consulting the female parent in a female-male partnership to notify family of classroom issues. Relatives planning for the next major holiday may default to reaching out only to the mother to arrange logistics. Let's get family and society on board with realizing dads can handle these obligations as well, for a more gender-equitable distribution of unpaid labor. Ask school to put the dad's contact information as the No. 1 contact. Especially if the extended family is on the dad's side, direct planning obligations fall to him. Let's break these gendered habits by recognizing and modifying them.

in the middle of a weekday with only 48 hours' notice. Many of us do not have the degree of flexibility in our work schedules to drop obligations with only 1- or 2-days' notice to attend such events, and many times, well-intentioned schools need a gentle reminder that not all families have a stay-at-home parent. We parents may not be able to make every classroom event parents are invited to, but we're doing great if we can attend 60% of them. Banish any parent guilt, and know that your son will know it's special on the days you *are* able to attend his school functions.

ROLE MODELING AS PARENTS

As my kids have grown through the years, in retrospect, I think I was a bit naive to think that because they had a physician mother, there were automatic gender-equity lessons being passed along. Both I and my kids' dad are MDs, but what message did we send when Mom did most of the driving to/from preschool, piano lessons, and swim lessons? What message was sent when Mom did most of the grocery shopping and meal prep? Were the messages we were sending in our daily lives consistent with the messaging I *wanted* to send them? I'm not so sure. In the hectic hustle of our daily lives, it was just easier for me to bear the brunt of running our home life, and at times, the big picture was lost in the details. Looking back, as partners we should have had more discussions about our global goals for the messaging we wanted to send the kids.

I asked one of my families specifically whether the parents had conversations about intentional parenting. For this family, Mom has been conscious and intentional about raising her sons with gender-equity awareness. She told me "Our boys learn by seeing, by witnessing the life we lead, by watching us share the responsibilities of running a household." She continued to tell me "Growing up, my dad drove us everywhere, and my mom always sat in the passenger seat. I'm intentional about letting my boys witness that sometimes I drive, sometimes their dad drives; let's make it normal." This seems like such a simple thing, doesn't it? But this mom's conscious choice literally put her in the driver's seat. Yes, our sons should witness us in the driver's seat when we're all on a journey together.

THE FAMILY JOURNEY

Delegate and Teach Navigation Skills

Toddlers and preschoolers can and should help around the home. Here are some examples of tasks that 2-, 3-, and 4-year-olds can help with around the house.

- Put toys away (Set up an egg timer and make it a fun "contest.")
- Fill the pet's food dish.
- Put dirty clothes into the laundry hamper.
- Wipe up spills.
- Dust furniture.
- Pile books.

Young kids who start chores at a young age develop a lifelong habit of helping around the home. Just as we teach our kids to brush their teeth twice a day for lifelong dental health, encouraging daily chores at an age-appropriate level will instill the habits and help our sons become better men.

Similar to what was discussed in Chapter 3, Nurturing Infants to Be Better Men, it is age appropriate for toddlers and preschool kids to go through phases in which they "prefer" one parent over the other. Your 3-year-old son may prefer one parent to give him his nighttime bath, share a mealtime, or read stories together. It's likely that one parent has performed these tasks with your son more than the other parent; however, make sure, when logistically feasible, to "swap roles" and mix which parent helps your son with which task. It's healthy and typical to, as a parent, have feelings of jealousy, inadequacy, or even relief when your child prefers his other parent. Know that these are usually short-lived phases, and the pendulum will eventually swing to the other parent once again. It's important for parents to be aware of this developmentally appropriate possibility because parents making a habit of mixing parenting jobs and roles will ensure an additional buffer against the tendency to fall into gendered parenting roles.

DISCIPLINE

As we coach our young boys about appropriate and inappropriate behaviors, the manner in which we communicate discipline to our sons matters. Some issues will be clear-cut (eg, if your child hits or bites another child); however, there are ways to communicate that nurture and support, rather than shame. There's a way to communicate that shows we are all working to be better, including adults.

The American Academy of Pediatrics encourages healthy forms of discipline such as positive reinforcement, limit setting, redirecting, and setting expectations. Physical spanking or hitting, or emotional shame or threats, do more harm than good. Spanking increases aggression in children and interferes with a healthy parent-child relationship. Physical discipline carries a risk of injuries, can lead to mental health problems, and, bottom line, does not work. Corporeal punishment over the long term leads to increased defiance and aggression over time.

There's a way to coach a child that doesn't fill them with shame. And when we adults ourselves misstep (we are human, and it's an inevitability), it's a teaching opportunity for our sons that we are all works in progress. No one is perfect; we all make mistakes—that includes our kids and ourselves. Relationship building for years to come recognizes the growth mindset for all of us.

THE CONCEPT OF CONSENT

In our goal of raising boys who will be better men, we need to start to define the concept of consent. To this end, preschool children can and should begin to learn anatomically correct terms to define body parts. This terminology includes *ears, mouth, elbows,* and, also, *penis* and *vagina*. When certain body parts are given nicknames that are frequently only family specific and not universally known, there is an unwritten message that these body parts are something to be ashamed about.

There's also a very practical reason to use the anatomically correct term for all body parts: in the unthinkable circumstance that your child could be subjected to abuse, even the youngest children need to be empowered with the proper language to accurately describe what occurred, involving which body parts.

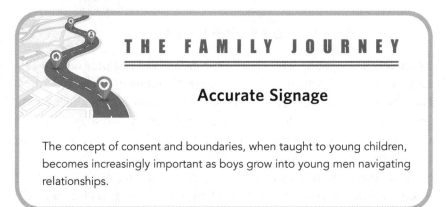

THE FAMILY JOURNEY

Accurate Signage

The concept of consent and boundaries, when taught to young children, becomes increasingly important as boys grow into young men navigating relationships.

In my clinical pediatrics practice, when I am examining a child 2 years or older for their yearly health supervision visit, I make an effort to model and coach the concept of consent for both the child and their parent. It usually leads to a fruitful conversation among all of us. For the examination, I work my way through in a head-to-toe fashion, first listening to the heart and lungs, then examining the ears, the mouth, and so on. When it's time to perform a genitourinary examination, I usually explain to the child "Part of your yearly head-to-toe exam is making sure the area covered by your underwear [or diaper/training pants] is healthy and developing correctly; it's only OK for the doctor to examine anything covered by a bathing suit if your grown-ups are here with you." Often parents are surprised by this narration, and they usually welcome it, as it can be an awkward topic to coach a child on what is and is not appropriate. My brief-and-to-the-point explanation with my patients, I hope, sets the stage for small but several ongoing conversations between parent and child about what is and is not appropriate for body parts, whether to look or to touch. The goal is for your young son, at age-appropriate ages and stages, to better learn about personal boundaries and recognize OK touch as compared with not-OK touch.

A family I spoke with has done a fair amount of research to learn to communicate the concept of consent to their 1-year-old son. These parents make a point to ask their son how he wants to say hello to, or goodbye to, friends and family. They do not make their son hug or kiss relatives; Mom pointed out that this was new for her family because she was always "required" to hug and kiss her grandmother. If their son indicates he doesn't feel comfortable with giving hugs, that is respected and honored. This empowers a young boy with autonomy over his choices.

At all ages, age-appropriate board books are an excellent way to share concepts and start discussions. Included at the end of this chapter are several resources for your family, including *Yes! No! A First Conversation About Consent* by Megan Madison and Jessica Ralli that can help get the ball rolling if you're feeling uncomfortable or unprepared to have these conversations.

Keep in mind that, while respecting boundaries, there is healthy touch. All kids need appropriate physical affection as they grow. Unfortunately, as our sons grow, appropriate physical touch often occurs less frequently. Appropriate physical touch can act as a buffer for stress and mental health struggles, and kids and adults, sons and men, need it.

WHAT IS TOXIC MASCULINITY?

Sonora Jha, PhD, media professor, writer, and feminist media scholar, defines *toxic masculinity* as "a cultural concept of manliness that glorifies stoicism, strength, virility, dominance, and violence, and that is socially maladaptive or harmful to boys' own mental health."[5] For our boys' sake, and for the sake of society and women, let's not expect our sons to be stoic, emotionless, or excessively independent.

---

5. Jha S. *How to Raise a Feminist Son: Motherhood, Masculinity, and the Making of Family.* Sasquatch Books; 2021.

Beyoncé spoke of raising her young son in an interview; even at an early age, "I want him to know that he can be strong and brave but that he can also be sensitive and kind. I want my son to have a high emotional IQ where he is free to be caring, truthful, and honest. It's everything a woman wants in a man, and yet we don't teach it to our boys."[6] I love that she draws a line between how we raise our sons and what kind of men we hope to witness and meet in this world. The road to healthy masculine traits begins in the toddler years.

INTERACTIONS WITH EXTENDED FAMILY OR THE GREATER COMMUNITY

Toddlers and preschoolers learn by playing. Young boys love to take part in imaginative play and to imitate the grown-ups around them. Boys and girls both enjoy building blocks and cars, and boys and girls both enjoy pretend-play cooking in a play kitchen, "restaurant," or cleaning. Some parents make sure they have lots of microfiber duster cloths on hand so their enthusiastic young kids can legitimately help tidy the home.

A family I spoke with who has a 3-year-old son shared with me that the grandfather solicited advice from the parents on what to get the boy for Christmas. The grandfather was dubious when the parents suggested a play kitchen, but he followed through on this suggestion. The boy's mom was thrilled when she saw that the kitchen set's box packaging featured exclusively boys playing with the set. That Christmas day now ranks among the family's favorite. The 3-year-old, with the help of his 9-year-old brother, worked all morning to transform the kitchen into a fast-food restaurant, spending the rest of the day delivering food to all their family members. Mom reflected on the day and said, "It was a great cross-generational moment." Their grandfather could clearly see how much the boys loved the new possibilities for creative play. Mom made a point to position the play kitchen in the dining area so it was convenient and accessible, and although actual meal prep happens in the real kitchen, her 3-year-old son is happily working alongside, in parallel, in his play kitchen.

---

6. Beyoncé. Beyoncé in her own words: her life, her body, her heritage. *Vogue*. August 6, 2018. Accessed May 17, 2023. https://www.vogue.com/article/beyonce-september-issue-2018.

The old notion of men being dominant and participating less frequently as caregivers is outdated. Former President Barack Obama has said in an interview, "No matter how enlightened a guy thinks he is, there's still a tilt in the direction of more burden falling on the woman." When asked whether this was a biological given or because of a dynamic playing out, Obama responded, "No, I think it's embedded in our social structures, in discrimination, in expectation, in messages that we're sending in the media and in entertainment."[7]

Grandparents and other family members may slip and falter in their comments and interactions. It's important to identify these areas and to call out (and call in) others (and ourselves) to do better. Especially if your son is the first grandchild, there is a shift in the family dynamic. I often remind the first-time parents in my practice to remember that *they* are the parents now, they are the ones in charge, and they can listen to and consider the advice of grandparents, but it's up to them what they try or how they decide to run their households. If after repeated scenarios, a grandparent is not showing a growth mindset or evidence of effort to learn or evolve, the parents must remember that their primary responsibility is to their child, to protect their child and to guide their child, so they should make decisions about family interactions accordingly.

Your son will begin to form friendships with neighbors and child care classmates. Encourage a diversity of relationships for your son. If your son happens to become friends with a girl, support this and avoid the prevalent temptation to label the relationship as romantic. Take the long view and imagine your son in 10, 20 years: it's healthy and appropriate to have platonic friendships with people who have a different gender. Some circles (kids *and* adults) still perpetuate a "cooties" myth for kids of other genders, and parents are wise to adopt a matter-of-fact, supportive stance on their son's preferred friendships. The same goes for friends whose parents' values may not align with your family's values. It may come to pass that your family becomes a safe haven for that friend. Keep an open mind and allow your son these initial stages of exploring relationships with others.

---

7. Shahani A. *Art of Power*. Barack Obama redefines what it means to be a man. May 13, 2021. Accessed May 17, 2023. https://www.wbez.org/stories/barack-obama-redefines-what-it-means-to-be-a-man/9cb514f8-7d89-43da-8912-b34399789771.

TEACHABLE MOMENTS

Consume Media Together

On the subject of media, the American Academy of Pediatrics recommends limiting screen time for our toddlers and preschoolers. When we do use media, we should use it selectively, choosing high-quality programming that is educational and nonviolent and, ideally, co-viewing it with our child to spark conversations and talk about what we're watching together.

Media has an undeniable force in our lives. Even something as seemingly innocuous as an NFL football game carries greater meaning for our young sons, as the only women on the field are typically the cheerleaders. I'm not saying don't watch football; I'm a big Chicago Bears fan (despite their record since the 1985 Super Bowl season). What I am suggesting is discussing what you observe, and balancing what your son is exposed to, when you witness these inequities. The most important media tip? Turn off the screen and head outside with your son. Media use *must* be balanced, and it is only one aspect of a larger lifestyle.

Common Sense Media (www.commonsensemedia.org) is an independent nonprofit organization that is a priceless resource for families with children of all ages. Their media reviews of television, films, video games, and more not only consider depictions of violent or sexual acts but also examine media for diversity and explore whether gender stereotypes are perpetuated. Bookmark this resource and consult it when your family is selecting media to view together. When you watch films that may or may not present a well-rounded viewpoint, point this out and talk about it. Help your sons digest what they're watching and put it into context of the real world.

Age-Appropriate Books and Media

When assessing media to share with your child, use the 3 Cs: content, context, and co-viewing. Keep the *content* age appropriate. Put the material into proper *context* for your child. *Co-view* with your son to keep communication and conversation going. Set the stage when your son is still at a young age to discuss a variety of topics.

Reading with your son has innumerable benefits for both of you. It promotes bonding, offers a great way to cuddle at the end of a long

THE FAMILY JOURNEY

Common Sense Media Statement on How Gender Stereotypes Affect Kids' Development

The concept of consent and boundaries, when taught to young children, becomes increasingly important as boys grow into young men navigating relationships.

What kids learn about gender at toddler and preschool ages

- They learn a traditional gender identity, specifically whether they are a girl or a boy.
- They learn stereotypes about activities, traits, toys, and skills that are linked to each gender.
- They develop and strengthen gender-typed play and activity preferences.
- They show a preference for playing with children of their own gender.

Goals for media content according to Common Sense Media

- Show kids with diverse attributes to show that there is more than one way to express and feel gender.
- Show portrayals that equally value boys and girls, masculine and feminine behaviors, and masculine and feminine characteristics.
- Show kids in a wide range of activities, including counter-stereotypical activities.
- Show girls and boys interacting in healthy and egalitarian cross-gender friendships.
- Show girls and boys of diverse races, body/facial/hair types, and clothes.
- Use a more gender-neutral palette.

Adapted from Ward LM, Aubrey JS. *Watching Gender: How Stereotypes in Movies and on TV Impact Kids' Development.* Common Sense Media; 2017.

day, may provide a cherished step in a consistent bedtime routine, and teaches early literacy skills. Significant to the goal of greater gender equity, reading with your son supports his development of a child's sense of empathy, putting themselves into another's (eg, a character's) point of view, and can initiate age-appropriate conversations about otherwise tricky subjects.

Suggested Books to Read With Your Toddler or Preschool Son

Codell R. *The Basket Ball*. Abrams Books for Young Readers; 2014. (Spoiler alert: Girls can play basketball!)

Cointreau M. *The Girl Who Could Dance in Outer Space: An Inspirational Tale About Mae Jemison*. Createspace Independent Publishing Platform; 2014.

Geeslin C. *Elena's Serenade*. Atheneum Books for Young Readers; 2004.

Gomi T. *My Friends*. Chronicle Books; 2005.

Leaf M. *The Story of Ferdinand*. Grosset & Dunlap; 1936. A bull would rather smell flowers than roughhouse.

Madison M, Ralli J. *Yes! No! A First Conversation About Consent*. Rise; 2022.

Munsch R. *The Paper Bag Princess*. Annick Press; 2018.

Newman L. *A Fire Engine for Ruthie*. Clarion Books; 2004. A girl loves playing with fire engines and motorcycles.

Parr T. *Be Who You Are*. Little, Brown & Co; 2016.

Parr T. *It's Okay to Be Different*. Little, Brown & Co; 2009.

WORDS MATTER: PHRASES AT STAGES THAT DO US NO FAVORS

The words we use matter. Words form thoughts and ideas, which then become reality. When a father engages in parenting activities, he is not "helping"; he is parenting. For example, don't let grandparents gush for an hour if Dad changes a dirty diaper in their presence unless Mom gets similar accolades for performing a similar task. No household or parenting chores are "mom duties"; they are parenting tasks. We've discussed avoiding the phrase "boys will be boys," but I'll state once again that this saying can quickly become a mindset leading to reality, to the detriment of not only what your boy feels he is capable of but also how society views your son. Certainly, your son is so much more than just his sex assigned at birth. He's a *person*.

Before you know it, your imaginative 4-year-old will be embarking on his school-age years. He'll spend most of his waking hours during the school year at school, and he'll have a variety of influences shaping his personal development and awareness of the world around him. The grade school years are a robust opportunity to communicate with your son, help him identify the feelings of others and himself, and help him become the future man, a whole person, that he will become.

RECOMMENDED RESOURCES FOR PARENTS OF TODDLER AND PRESCHOOL BOYS

@biglittlefeelings. Accessed May 17, 2023. https://www. instagram.com/BigLittleFeelings. Although you should always be selective in the social media you follow for child advice, this page is a pediatrician-approved approach with tangible steps and practical tips to better communicate with your children aged 1 to 6 years.

Forehead R, Long N. *Parenting the Strong-willed Child: The Clinically Proven Five-Week Program for Parents of Two- to Six-Year-Olds*. 3rd ed. McGraw-Hill; 2010. A tried-and-true resource for families that realize that crafting an appropriate behavior framework is 80% positive reinforcement and 20% consequences. Perfect for busy working families, the book lays out a manageable plan, divided over 5 weeks, and recognizes the need to preserve a child's self-esteem within the discipline framework to better manage young children's behavior.

Chapter 5

Nurturing School-aged Boys to Be Better Men: Expanding Our Sons' Scope to School and Community

When my oldest son was a college student in his second year home for winter break, the COVID-19 pandemic was still raging. Because we still weren't traveling or socializing in large groups, we figured this was a great time to go through all the "memory boxes" stored in his childhood bedroom closet. Background: As my kids grew, whenever I wasn't sure where to store a childhood artwork, craft, or project, one deemed too important for the trash, I either snapped a digital photo of it or tossed it into a growing box in each kid's closet (which then multiplied into a few boxes, despite my claims to be a minimalist). The cumulative effect has been at least a couple of memory boxes in each of my kids' closets, each overflowing with childhood mementos. Some of the stored items were hilarious, some were endearing, and some left us scratching our heads and asking "*Why* exactly did we save this?"

MEMORY BOXES

My son and I were equal parts cracking up with laughter and baffled, digging through these memories together. He frequently pulled out his phone to document items both to keep for himself and to share with his college friends; I pulled a stapled 8 × 10–inch office-paper project out of the box. The spring of my son's third-grade year, his teacher had the classroom students complete a *Mother's Day Magazine*. The cover of

the "magazine" is emblazoned with a hand drawing of me, the price tag states "Priceless," and the featured headline states "Shelly Flais, Chosen Mother-Of-The-Year." Page 1 is titled "INTERVIEW: My Mother is the Best!" accompanied by another (rather hilarious) drawing of me (I pray I didn't actually look like that to him when he was 9 years old):

As enlightened as we parents all think ourselves to be, when we think about third-grade boys, do we usually consider that they will love cooking in the kitchen with their mom? I personally happen to love cooking, and I have to admit, each time I incorporated my kids into food shopping and food prep (which was pretty frequently, as it turns out a family needs to eat dinner every night), I wasn't mindfully executing gender-equitable parenting goals. We were just spending time together engaging in a necessary life task that I happen to enjoy doing. And that's just it, isn't it? Let's share what we love with our kids, and let's allow our kids be whole people, without "pre-editing" the interests and activities we share together, regardless of gender.

When I ask the grade school patients in my pediatrics clinical practice what they like to cook in their home kitchen, often I get to hear about great new recipes, but in equal measure, I'm met with blank stares or even a visual moment on the parent's face of "We didn't even think of that." Food is life; we all need it for daily sustenance, so encouraging our sons and daughters to spend time with us in the kitchen is not only fostering important life skills (everyone has to eat after all) but also setting the stage for more equitable sharing of household tasks in the future when the kids are adults. (Sidenote: I've always found it ironic that cooking and meal prep have historically been household tasks assigned to women, yet in the professional culinary world, restaurant head chefs are overwhelmingly men. What a dichotomy. That fact alone shows that the ability to cook is not a skill defined by gender lines.)

Most important is simply spending time together engaged in a pleasant activity. Pediatricians love the expression "meet your child where they are." Your son isn't a big fan of cooking or baking? No problem. What *does* he enjoy? It speaks volumes to your son how important your relationship is if you engage in *his* favorite activities, and it boosts his self-esteem to realize that you care about what he's interested in. So, you don't have a clue about Minecraft... No problem. In fact, even better, because *he* can show *you* what to do. What a powerful message it can be that your son has expert skills he can teach others. A parent allowing their son to teach them also models a flexible, growth mindset for our sons: so we screw up and flounder in the early stages, no big deal! Let's model resilience for our sons as we laugh at our own foibles seeking to understand a new activity.

KIDS RISE TO EXPECTATIONS

In raising school-aged children, we must be aware that kids rise to expectations. Perception becomes reality. If we as parents have a closed view of who our sons are, and what they're capable of, we'll define a box that limits their growth and individuality. It's so important for us as parents and partners to widen our views and expectations of who our sons are and could be.

When I was in fourth grade, I was identified for and placed into an academically gifted program. One of the weekly activities was "mind bender" puzzles. I'd bring these home and my dad would regularly sit with me to work on these, just as he had with my older brothers when they were my age. I am grateful that he knew his daughter would benefit from that time as well. Looking back on this as an adult, I'm sure a big reason my dad loved this activity was that he enjoyed the puzzles in and of themselves, and that is perfectly OK! His passion for the puzzles was palpable, and what a great message we send our kids when we share what we love with them. The key is that we had shared parent-child time engaging in a fun, growth-promoting activity, irrespective of the fact that I was a daughter and not a son. I felt special and especially proud when I made step-by-step progress in each puzzle, feeling his pride as he sat next to me. Working on these puzzles together remains one of my most cherished childhood memories of my dad.

Although parents and the immediate family remain predominant influences in a boy's life, the grade school years of development are shaped by new relationships and social interactions with individuals outside the family unit. Friends, classmates, teachers, extracurricular leaders, and youth sports coaches all start to play increasing roles in our sons' formative years. Although these relationships can serve as profoundly meaningful, positive interactions, unfortunately, there may also be less-than-ideal interactions. You'll witness situations that foster the status quo and limit how boys are defined, what emotions boys are allowed to have and convey, and the role boys play in their relationships with family, friends, peers, teammates, and the outside world. In addition to these outside relationships, media, including television, film, video games, and social media, plays an increased role in how our sons view themselves and how they interact with the world around them.

DAILY INTERACTIONS PROVIDE COMMUNICATION OPPORTUNITIES

A hallmark of a boy's school-age years is increased time in the school environment. During the school year, much of school-aged kids' waking hours are spent at school, away from parents and the family environment, and it is an adjustment for all parties involved, kid and adult alike. As a son navigates this new domain, it is important for both partners to continually check in on their son's growing emotional life.

Many parents tell me their sons are not as eager to share their daily events with family in the evenings in the same manner as their daughters (Certainly, there are many households in which sons are forthcoming and daughters are not!). I discourage a strategy of barraging your child with a game of Twenty Questions. Asking "How was your day?" or other such limiting questions often leads to yes-or-no answers. Your goal as a parent is to have *conversations*.

Finding Opportunities to Talk

I have found that the best way to talk with my sons about anything and everything is to chat *while doing other things*. Whether doing household chores such as sorting laundry or setting the table, going for a simple neighborhood walk after dinner, or playing 10 minutes of catch outside with a kid, it's often a great strategy for parents to simply be quiet and let the conversation happen organically. Similarly, car rides are a great way to talk with our kids; removing the somewhat intense element of eye contact can help younger kids open up. Taking the scenic route, allowing your son to share what is on his mind, is a great opportunity. A key element of spontaneous conversation in general is minimizing screen time, for us adults and for our kids. A car full of kids "zombied out" on screens won't allow for fruitful conversation.

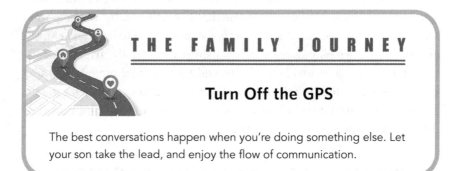

THE FAMILY JOURNEY

Turn Off the GPS

The best conversations happen when you're doing something else. Let your son take the lead, and enjoy the flow of communication.

If and when your son opens up and mentions a current event or issue from his life, resist the temptation to verbally and immediately jump in. Let him steer the conversation. Active listening such as nodding, saying "I see," or saying "That must have been fun/stressful/upsetting" demonstrates your interest and engagement without taking over the discussion. It also gives parents an opportunity to help their son identify his feelings. The key point here is to help your son feel heard and to keep up the momentum of communication. Avoid voicing excessive judgment; often, your son will already be able to identify good and not-so-good choices himself, but more importantly, if he's feeling judged, he may not want to open up to you the next time.

A strategy that works for a lot of ages (including adults) is "highs and lows" (or, alternatively, "apples and onions"). Your son can share the best and worst moments of his day, and you should also. This is especially great for bedtime conversations, when tucking in your son for the night. What was the best part of the day? What was the not-so-great part of the day? It's OK if there are multiple great parts; the point is not what the actual highs and lows are. The point is *communication,* a conversation, learning more about each other. These conversations help kids develop empathy, as well as normalize resilience when they watch us deal with our own adult inconveniences and challenges.

Talk About Screen Time

Screens (eg, smartphones, tablets, televisions) are prevalent and can inhibit spontaneous conversation. It's a great idea to have a family philosophy about screen time to promote communication and to support the healthy emotional lives of our kids. Partners should not only talk with each other to be on similar pages about their expectations but also hold each other accountable to lead by a good example, monitoring their own screen use. Mealtimes should be screen-free. Car rides of less than 30 minutes can easily be screen-free. No parent ever regretted waiting longer to allow their child to have a personal smartphone. Here's an analogy I share with my patients' families: it's easier to open a door slowly than to yank the door wide open and then, later, have to dial it back. Similarly, if and when you deem your child ready for a smartphone, the initial stages of having the phone should be enforced with time restraints, loosened over time with appropriate use and increasing maturity.

Do you feel that your family has already gone overboard with personal screens? The pandemic and switch to online learning didn't help. Additionally,

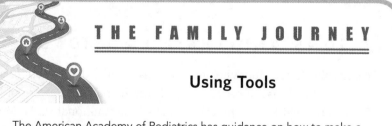

THE FAMILY JOURNEY

Using Tools

The American Academy of Pediatrics has guidance on how to make a Family Media Use Plan on HealthyChildren.org at www.healthychildren. org/English/family-life/Media/Pages/How-to-Make-a-Family-Media-Use-Plan.aspx, including an interactive tool to more easily create a personalized plan tailored to your specific needs and goals.

we adults need to be self-aware of our own screen use. It's the height of hypocrisy to scold kids' screen use if we're constantly checking notifications or answering work emails ourselves. Parents need to model what they want their kids to do and to discuss screen mindfulness with their kids. Just as we fuel our bodies with healthful foods in appropriate portions, media consumption should be healthful content in appropriate amounts. After a busy night taking patient calls for my pediatric practice, I'm all too eager the next day to show my kids I'm powering off my phone and putting it away for a few hours to regain sanity. I tell them "Don't text me—come find me and talk with me if you've got something to say!" Whether just a few hours or even longer, a period of going cold turkey without screens can help reset everyone's thermostats. The summer months are ideal for 1 week's or even 1 month's time of no screens. My patients' families that have used this approach are pleasantly surprised to report that oftentimes the kids realize they don't even miss the screens.

THE FAMILY JOURNEY

Creative Route

Screen time inhibits communication. Flip the script and join your son in a video game. Be judicious with screen time, but know you can also use it to bond with your son.

SONS AND THEIR EMOTIONS

Good communication includes helping our sons identify their emotions and feelings, as well as those of others. Schools are increasingly aware of the need for school-aged kids to practice their social-emotional skills. Many public-school districts have a version of social-emotional learning starting as early as kindergarten, with a teacher-led session of 15 minutes per day to help kids connect words to their emotions and develop empathy for others.

In my preparations for writing this book, I made a point to connect with families of boys of all ages. One mom of a fourth grader pointed out, regarding grade school boys, that we need to help our sons "feel the feelings; you've got to go through [your feelings] to get to the other side of it." Our daughters may be more forthcoming with daily school events, but it's equally important for our sons to be able to express themselves. This mom pointed out, "Sometimes you need a good cry; get it out of your system, take a deep breath, and then go do what you have to do." This message is equally important to hear from dads. Many of us adults are still learning these lessons ourselves.

TOYS SHAPE GENDER IDENTITY

The toys a boy plays with shape his gender identity and foster his role interacting with others. Are you open-minded about the toys and items your sons and daughters can use or should receive as gifts? Jordan Shapiro writes in his book *Father Figure:*

> When we walked through…big box retailers, I regularly made remarks about the absurdity of toys being divided into pink and blue aisles. What could possibly make a particular LEGO set more appealing to one gender than another?…Sometimes other adults would give me sideways glances, or roll their eyes. They thought I was spoiling the children's fun. Let them have their muscly superheroes and pink princesses; they like it, don't ruin it for them! The implication was that little kids deserved a childhood free from social-justice concerns. I knew that was just plain wrong. Ubiquitous gender stereotypes are way more oppressive to a child's naivete than any acknowledgement of misogyny, homophobia, or transphobia could ever be.[1]

Be mindful of the pervasive nature of the concept of gendered toys. You can coach your kids by simply sharing that "There are no 'girl things' and 'boy things.' Both boys and girls can do/like/wear XYZ." This motto will help your kids internalize the message.

I would argue that as Americans, we have too much stuff in general. Many families, if opting to hold birthday parties for their child, wish to avoid a barrage of gifts that will go unused or add to landfills. An alternative to gifts is to ask for charitable donations, or for wrapped presents to take to a local children's hospital to give to the patients. An idea I've implemented over the years is that in lieu of a big, chaotic, expensive, stressful party, my child chooses 1 or 2 special friends for an experience, which aligns

---

1. Shapiro J. *Father Figure: How to Be a Feminist Dad.* Little, Brown Spark; 2021.

with our core value of "experiences, not things." Ideas have ranged from enjoying a penguin encounter at the local aquarium, to inviting a couple of friends to attend a college football game together, to inviting a couple of friends to join us for a fancy tea service in a city hotel.

EXTRACURRICULAR ACTIVITIES AND SPORTS

Impact

Extracurricular activities take up increased importance in a school-aged boy's life. Musical instruments, scouting, religious groups, sports, cultural clubs, volunteering ... You'll have plenty of options. Have open conversations with your sons about what they're interested in trying and, just as importantly, why they may not want to continue with an activity they've participated in. Chorus, violin, theater, piano—please offer these options to your sons and don't be dismayed if they're the rare boy in a sea of girls; what matters most is their interest level in, passion for, and engagement with the activity.

School-aged kids are experimenting with a variety of youth sports. You'll be surprised not only at the range of options but also at the range of attitudes and messages from the coaches, other parents, and adult organizers. The youth sport industry has become a juggernaut over the years. When done well, youth sports are age-appropriate, emotionally healthy places for our kids to engage in physical and mental exercise, grow as individuals, learn the concept of teamwork, and broaden their social scope beyond that of the classroom. Pay attention and ensure that your son's activities support these goals.

THE FAMILY JOURNEY

Choose a Route

Twenty-first century youth sports can be overwhelming and, in many cases, are much different from the casual rec leagues we may have grown up with ourselves. Whether sports or extracurricular activities in general, ensure that your son's influences support your big-picture goals of promoting gender equity.

THE FAMILY JOURNEY

Alternative Routes

Families often have a limited budget, but that need not limit out-of-school opportunities. Your local public library likely offers arts and crafts, book clubs, movie nights, and more; browse the library website to explore offerings. YMCAs offer lower-cost swim lessons, gymnastics, and soccer camps. Boys & Girls Clubs offer drama, photography, art, music, and science. Youth programs bring a diversity of people into your son's world, a key stepping stone toward empathy of, and allyship with, others.

Messaging

Pay close attention to the messaging, attitudes, and culture of the sports that your kids are dabbling in. All too often, the focus is on the financial viability of the club sport instead of age-appropriate nurturing of the kids participating. Coaches with old-school mentalities (eg, telling third-grade boys in flag football to "Man up") may lead the teams. As parents, we do have power. We are our kids' best advocates, and if your son's sports team is promoting unhealthy patterns, gender-equity related or otherwise, speak up. The best coaches will have a growth mindset and use the scenario as a learning opportunity. Conversely, if your son's coaches have inflexible, fixed mindsets, and your issue is not addressed but instead derided, you still have power: you have the power to remove your kid from that particular team. If this approach is taken, it's often a good message to your son to "finish what you started" by completing the season with the existing team before making the move elsewhere. Lots of open conversations with your son about what is happening, and why a switch may be healthy, are a great idea, as you want your son to understand and be on board with any necessary changes, especially if he's formed friendships on that team.

A personal note: My 3 sons and 1 daughter participated in club swim for years growing up. As a pediatrician, I loved that club swim promoted water safety and life skills. We live with cold Chicago winters, and thanks to indoor pools, year-round exercise is possible. Swimming is also a sport that can be considered gender equitable: boys and girls compete with themselves to improve their times, boys and girls can equally crush their goals, and there are many instances in which the girls swim faster than the boys! Please consider a swim team if it is a local option for your family. Martial arts are another example of a non-gendered physical activity that can be enjoyed during cold winters: win-win-win.

ROLE MODELING AS PARENTS

Partners should model gender equity for their school-aged son by sharing the tasks of running the household. It won't be an even 50-50; some household domains are 70-30, whereas other domains are 30-70. The point is that there is *overall* balance and equity. For example, if one partner takes on outdoor or car maintenance tasks (eg, changing the car's oil), the other partner can take on indoor tasks (eg, doing laundry or cooking). A key part of chores is having your kids help with the task in an age-appropriate manner (even if that means your son is simply observing and handing you tools from time to time). These are the routine life events in which you're spending time with your son, chatting all the while, passing on skills, and, I hope, sharing a couple of laughs along the way.

Involving your son in these household-maintenance tasks can seem like more work for you in the short run, but in the long run, you'll all reap the rewards of better life skills and a teenager who actually knows how to snow blow your driveway the next time it snows a foot, or who can replace burned out lightbulbs without assistance. As my own teenagers got older, I maintained a kitchen philosophy of "you can cook whatever you like, as long as you clean it up." It's a good habit to get into from day one, and besides, any good cook cleans as they go. Also, selfishly, I love cooking yet cannot stand the cleanup.

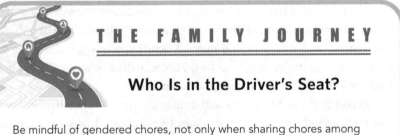

THE FAMILY JOURNEY

Who Is in the Driver's Seat?

Be mindful of gendered chores, not only when sharing chores among partners but also when assigning chores to your sons and daughters.

Caregiving Labor

Separate from household daily tasks, the distribution of the *caregiving* labor should be as equitable as possible. Over the years, each partner will have particular challenges or stages in their own careers, and there will be times when partners "take turns" supporting each other's goals and, correspondingly, take the helm on caregiving for that stretch. Ongoing conversations between partners are vital to reassess and realign roles as needed. Former President Barack Obama stated in an NPR interview, "Broadening the definition [of how we think about men] so that we're telling our boys 'You being a good caregiver is part of what you should be as a man because it's part of what you should be as an adult.' Right? Showing compassion is not weakness. Listening is as important as talking."[2] Men: Model these skills so your son can see that any of us can, and should, be caregivers.

Household Tasks: Shared-Between Parent-Kid Teamwork

Grade schoolers, boys and girls alike, should absolutely have chores. Teaching our sons to independently handle day-to-day tasks sets the stage for years to come. Kids at this age should be able to advance and sort laundry, set the table at mealtimes, load the dishwasher and start it (if they can play Minecraft, they can turn on a dishwasher), shred papers, and take out the garbage, as just a few examples. Each morning, your son should take increased ownership over the tasks needed to get ready to start the new school day, such as making a simple breakfast for himself, brushing his teeth, gathering his supplies, and readying his backpack, without constant reminders from a parent. If your son is not a morning person, consider moving some of these steps to the evening hours the night before. These tasks not only help you run each day more smoothly but also help your son develop the important executive functioning skill of planning his day.

Glennon Doyle shares a vulnerable parenting moment in her 2020 book, *Untamed,* regarding her son and household chores. She realized a shift was needed as she was picking up after her son, who had a busy schedule of school and sports. One day, her son didn't finish his list of chores, citing a physics test the next day. Her response?

---

2. Shahani A. *Art of Power.* Barack Obama redefines what it means to be a man. May 13, 2021. Accessed May 16, 2023. https://www.wbez.org/stories/barack-obama-redefines-what-it-means-to-be-a-man/9cb514f8-7d89-43da-8912-b34399789771.

I said, "No, *I'm sorry,* Chase. I've been sending you the wrong message. I have accidentally taught you that achieving out there is more important than serving your family in here. I've taught you that home is where you spend your leftover energy, out there is where you give your best. I need to course-correct by giving you this bottom line: I don't give a rat's ass how much respect you earn for yourself out in the world if you are not showing respect to the people inside your home. If you don't get that right, nothing you do out there will matter much." Our boys are born with great potential for nurturing, caring, loving, and serving. Let's stop training it out of them.[3]

As parents, we will make mistakes. Recognize those moments, adapt, and communicate.

THE FAMILY JOURNEY

Each Team Member Plays a Role

School-aged kids can and should participate in household chores. Caring for lived spaces is *everyone's* job. Boys who grow up participating in the care of the home grow into men who participate in the care of a home. Chores can include

- Make their bed.
- Empty wastebaskets.
- Bring in mail.
- Set the mealtime table, and clear the table after a meal.
- Pull weeds in the yard.
- Use a handheld vacuum to clean up crumbs.
- Water flowers.
- Unload the dishwasher (melamine, nonbreakable plates are great for this).
- Wash unbreakable dishes at the sink.
- Fix a bowl of cereal.
- Sort laundry.
- Sweep floors.
- Help make and pack lunch.

---

3. Doyle G. *Untamed.* Dial Press; 2020.

- Rake leaves in the yard.
- Keep their bedroom tidy.

After 8 years old, kids can do all the above and

- Load the dishwasher.
- Help put away groceries.
- Vacuum.
- Help make dinner.
- Make their own breakfast or snacks.
- Wash the table after a meal.
- Put away their own laundry.
- Take the pet for a walk.

Partners might not share the same philosophies when it comes to kids taking on household chores or when it comes to how much responsibility the child should take in their own personal care, whether getting ready for school, an extracurricular activity or sport, or bedtime. Open conversations between partners, between separated parents, and with the family as a whole are required in these situations. For 2-household families, it's OK to have slightly different routines. If you're not living with your son's other parent, know that the rules, traditions, and expectations you establish with your son *will* "stick."

As discussed in previous chapters, be mindful of who prepares what for special days. Consider holidays, birthdays, and major family events: Who is cooking? Who is serving the food? Who is cleaning up after? Model for your son what you want to happen in his future, and enlist his eager help to set the stage for years of celebrations to come.

THE FAMILY CALENDAR

Whether you use technology and apps or an old-school, large paper calendar centralized in your home (ours is in the kitchen), make sure you have some version of an agreed-on system for family logistics. School holidays and vacations, special events at school, pediatric appointments, visits from extended family—all the adults in the house should be on the same page about logistics management. Additionally, school-aged boys are developmentally ready to be aware of and to navigate the executive function skills of being aware of their own school and extracurricular schedule.

Our Family Calendar

Sunday	Monday	Tuesday	Wednesday	Thursday	Friday	Saturday
18	19	20	21	22	23	24
9:00 am religious education	After-school chess tournament	3:00 pm piano lesson		9:00 am oil change—Who will take car??	Grocery shopping (Plan a menu for the week)	

THE FAMILY JOURNEY

Charting a Course

School-aged boys are now at an age when they can actively participate in the family calendar and can contribute to the teamwork. Our sons can now check out library books, attend birthday parties, or attend after-school activities; as such, they are active contributors to the calendar. One suggestion is to color-code items by kids or themes. There will be a learning curve with coaching and review from adults to help their son's progress. Start simple with your son, adding a friend's birthday party to the calendar. As your son grows, his responsibility to the shared family calendar will also grow.

All too often, the female parent in a female-male partnership is the gatekeeper of family logistics and the knowledge bearer of everyone's comings and goings. It doesn't promote gender equity to have a single parent disproportionately sharing this burden. At times, we hear a parent overly dependent on reminders say "Oh I didn't know" and this just isn't acceptable; we are all fully functional adults. As an example, frequently moms are the ones who rearrange work when there's a random Monday school holiday. Let's promote gender equity and let sons watch as dads shuffle work obligations to ensure child care for those random days off of school. Our boys are always watching, and we can model for them to become better men.

SCHOOL COMMUNICATION

Your son's grade school will likely have some system for notifying the family if your son gets sick at school or if there are classroom or peer issues. The default setting will probably be to call your son's mom if you are in a female-male partnership. *Communicate* with school staff and make sure the dad's contact information is high on the phone tree listing. Communicate with your partner and decide who should be available to answer calls and texts during school hours, for the inevitability that there will be an issue with your son during those hours. Happily, in my clinical pediatrics practice, when I'm clarifying with parents contact information to call a family back with test results, dads will often say "Oh, that's Mom's cell, but she's at work, so please call me instead." Similarly, I make a point to make sure my patients' fathers have patient portal access to their child's medical chart. I know that dads want to receive communication from not only the doctor but also the school.

Have an important, can't-be-interrupted meeting? Arrange for coverage during that time, but it doesn't promote gender equity if one of the parents shields themselves from parental obligations because "I have work." We are *all* working, whether it's inside or outside the household. What is most important is the messaging, and it speaks volumes if a son vomits at school, he needs to be picked up, and his dad is the one to swoop in, save the day, and take care of him.

Special events will come up at school. One of my boys had a poetry slam in fourth grade, and I still remember my heartbreak when the classroom parents' first notification of and invitation to attend this classroom event was only 2 days prior. Of course, I had a fully booked clinic of patient visits scheduled, and it's not possible to alter my work schedule with such short notice. All too often, the default setting for schools is the assumption that families have a flexible-schedule parent or a stay-at-home parent, and this is simply not the case in the 21st century. I can't believe I have to type this, but my personal experiences interacting with my 4 kids' schools over the years tells me I must.

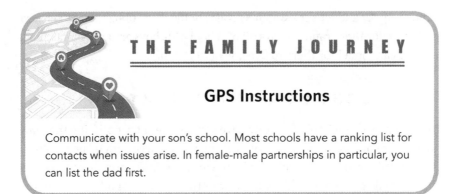

THE FAMILY JOURNEY

GPS Instructions

Communicate with your son's school. Most schools have a ranking list for contacts when issues arise. In female-male partnerships in particular, you can list the dad first.

Each new academic year, email your kids' teachers to let them know that work schedules need at least 1 to 2 weeks' notice for special school functions, field trips, and other programming that may require parent time. Most teachers and educators welcome this communication and work to create an inclusive environment that supports working parents. And of course, there will be field trips that you simply cannot miss work to chaperone, but with advance notice, the other parent or another trusted adult, such as a grandparent, can attend in your absence. Let's normalize the diversity of working-parent families to support our kids in the school environment and promote gender equity.

Use your son's interactions with classmates as teachable moments, even the unpleasant ones. A family with a fourth grader shared this experience with me: "Among a group of 6 boys who formed a friend group, one of the other boy's moms emailed me, stating that my son had been bullying her son for weeks. My partner and I were shocked. This information came out of nowhere. Our son earned high report card grades and did not have disciplinary issues at school, nor did we get word of any problems from the teachers. My partner and I asked each other 'How do we approach this?' We made the decision together to have our son read the email for himself so he could see what was being said. Clearly, the other child had different boundaries than our son." This situation led to greater discussions of truth telling and trust, trust as a concept between son and parent and trust as a concept between our sons and their peers. His mom reinforced to him that "This is a motto for our family this year: If someone shows you who they are, believe them."

This scenario goes beyond the issue of trust between peers and parents and sons. The boy in this scenario happened to be a boy of color. This mom felt frustrated and asked the school administrators the greater questions of managing expectations and establishing credibility. This mom deservedly wanted to know whether anyone could suggest any scenario without proof. It's difficult to prove a negative or to prove the absence of something. This mom felt it became increasingly important to have conversations with her son about being mindful and cautious to ensure neither his actions nor his intentions were misconstrued. The scenario is a sad reminder that not all fourth-grade children are held to the same standards or given the same benefit of the doubt. Discussing these circumstances with your son will expand his worldview and help shape him as a man.

COMMUNICATION AND EMOTIONAL LITERACY

It's not only OK for boys to talk but also a necessary, healthy way for boys to expand their emotional literacy. A mom of a fifth-grade boy who I spoke with felt that "it's taboo for boys to talk." If your son tends to be less verbally communicative, do you find yourself surprised on the days he opens up to you? How do you respond in these moments? Are you able to put your current task on pause to allow your son to feel heard?

Or alternatively, do we subconsciously squash the moments when our sons open up to us (all too easy to do in our overscheduled lives with constant pulls for our attention)? If our sons are emotional about something that happened with a sibling or at school, do we reflexively send a message of "I can't deal with this right now," to suck it up and move on? If a son's communication is consistently shut down, his self-esteem can be eroded; just as important, these are lost opportunities for identifying emotions, for your son and for those he interacts with, and for instilling empathy. Additionally,

THE FAMILY JOURNEY

Read the Map

How to communicate more effectively with your son? Talk less. Listen more. Boys who feel heard have higher self-esteem and grow into better men.

if he feels that sharing his emotions is a nuisance to others, the next time something comes up, he may preemptively close the door on communication.

A fair amount of self-awareness is needed here, and certainly, I am not perfect in this respect. We are all works in progress. But it's important for parents to be introspective, assess our willingness to listen, and make sure our sons have a safe space to tell us things. Often parents do *too much talking,* plain and simple. If you have an issue with talking too much, consider even glancing at a clock and quietly letting your son "have the floor" for at least 2 to 3 minutes before interjecting, asking follow-up questions, or offering solutions and suggestions. You might be surprised at where the conversation takes you when we as adults don't immediately jump in. It can be helpful to ask your son "Would you like to vent and just talk about it, or would you like me to help you with suggestions or solutions?" You might be surprised because often school-aged kids, when given the chance to express themselves, arrive at pretty good ideas themselves, all on their own. It's also a great self-esteem booster to tell your son "I trust your judgment."

It's so important during the grade school years that we support our sons as they explore empathy for others. The Golden Rule, Treat others the way you wish to be treated, cannot be overstated. Let's face it, as we navigate adult life, we can find that many *adults* need a reminder of the Golden Rule. Model empathy as a parent. Seek out activities and athletics that are run by grown-ups who exhibit this important character trait. Parents need to take tangible steps to help their son "flex" his empathy muscles. Psychologists Dan Kindlon, PhD, and Michael Thompson, PhD, write in *Raising Cain:*

> There are many ways to give boys the opportunity to learn to be empathetic. Tending pets is one way. Tending people and tending community is another. Boys of all ages need the chance to take care of animals, babies, the needy, older people, the environment. We see boy empathy in schools where community service programs are a regular part of the curriculum; we see boy empathy in families where brothers and sisters need care and help.[4]

When we keep the character trait of empathy at the front of our minds, our sons are more well-rounded and everyone wins.

Michael Ian Black, the comedian, writes in his book *A Better Man:*

> Traditional masculinity encourages strength, independence, fortitude. All good qualities. At the same time, though, it provides no useful outlets for

---

4. Kindlon D, Thompson M. *Raising Cain: Protecting the Emotional Life of Boys.* Ballantine Books; 1999.

our vulnerability. If we cannot allow ourselves vulnerability, how are we supposed to experience wonder, fear, tenderness? If we cannot turn to others for help, what do we do with bewilderment and frustration? How do we even express something as elemental as joy?[5]

The idea that a boy, to evolve into a mature man, needs to be a lone wolf is incomplete. Connection, friendship, and community help our boys retain empathy and vulnerability.

Years ago, I heard an incredible piece of parenting advice that I've worked hard to live by: "When you hug your child, never be the first one to let go." Our sons may be getting older, but they still need our emotional support as they grow through developmental stages. If your son is comfortable with physical affection, keep hugs as part of your daily routine. Sidenote: If you choose to share this sage wisdom with them, as I eventually did, don't be surprised if you're subjected to marathon hug sessions. "Competitive" children love extending the hug to test whether you can truly abide by the "never be the first one to let go" advice, mimicking a staring contest of affectionate proportions.

THE FAMILY JOURNEY

Different Kinds of Signs

Communication consists of spoken words, as well as unspoken cues. Making eye contact, putting down what you're doing to listen, and providing a loving embrace can say just as much as actual words can. Model these skills to your son, and when he uses different ways to communicate with you, help him feel heard.

DISCIPLINE AND UNINTENDED CONSEQUENCES

The word *discipline* is derived from the Latin word for "instruction," or "knowledge." As a pediatrician, I often remind the families in my clinical

---

5. Black MI. *A Better Man: A (Mostly Serious) Letter to My Son.* Algonquin Books of Chapel Hill; 2020.

pediatrics practice that proper discipline means you're *teaching* your child about an appropriate framework of behavior. All too often, the word *discipline* is equated with the word *punishment,* which is unfortunate, as 80% of effective discipline is positive reinforcement when things are going well, with only 20% being redirection or limit setting when things aren't going well. The best methods of discipline include positive reinforcement, the setting of future expectations, and limit setting.

The American Academy of Pediatrics stance is clear on the subject of spanking or other forms of corporal punishment. Spanking, hitting, slapping, insulting, or humiliating a child can irrevocably affect the parent-child relationship and is linked to aggressive behavior in children. Research shows that it doesn't even work: corporal punishment makes it *more* likely that the child will display defiance in the future. Sadly, life stressors such as the COVID-19 pandemic, job loss, or substance use/use disorder can increase the use of excessively harsh punishments.[6] Unfortunately, spanking is often a gendered form of punishment. Research shows corporal punishment is more frequently administered to boys. This phenomenon in turn harms our sons and has negative effects for years to come.

As boys tend to be on the receiving end of a greater degree of physical punishments, a generations-long trend of boys and men shutting down, avoiding unpleasant emotions, is perpetuated. Drs Kindlon and Thompson write:

> Where we see harsh discipline or abuse in boys' lives, we see boys who struggle with shame, self-hatred, and anger. Many boys simply shut down emotionally at a young age and stay that way, unable to understand or express their feelings as they move into adult relationships in work, marriage, and family. Deeply shamed, sad, and angry boys don't just get over it with the passage of time. We know because we work with the angry, anxious, or depressed men so many of them grow up to be.[7]

Even if it was how you were raised, corporal punishment is a disproven method of discipline that needs to stop.

We parents are human, and we *will* have moments of anger; in the heat of the moment, count to 10, give yourself space to cool off, and even consider a self-imposed time-out. If you find yourself consistently out of control when disciplining your child, talk with your primary care provider and explore your options, including counseling or therapy, to better regulate your emotions. If you're not sure where to start, ask your son's pediatrician.

MALE ALLYSHIP

In the spirit of modeling behaviors that we want to witness in our kids, parents, especially dads, should point out women's successes at every opportunity. Discussion is merited all the more if women's accomplishments are diminished (or even forgotten!) in comparison to the discussion of men's successes.

Debbie Wosskow, UK-based entrepreneur, and author, posted a succinct story of male allyship to her social media:

Presenter: You're the first person to win two Olympic gold medals for tennis.

Andy Murray: I think Venus and Serena have won about four each.

Reporter: Querrey is the first US player to reach a major semifinal since 2009.

Andy Murray: Male player.

The solidarity that Andy Murray shows to the Williams sisters, and the space he continues to create for them, is exactly what it means to be a male ally.

It's not just on women to do all the work.

It's not just on women to create their own seat at the table.

It's not just on women to fight to be heard.

Male allies are so important. We need to see men who want women to win—and can take the highs and lows alongside them.

We need to see fathers of daughters, evangelists, supporters, investors, and sponsors, all taking up space and raising the voices of the women around them.

(continued on next page)

> Being pro-woman doesn't mean being anti-man.
>
> It's on all of us to make the change.
>

Fathers should model this behavior and mindset with their sons. Attend your son's older female cousin's softball game. Talk about the neighbor female classmate whose artwork was featured in a community program. Celebrate the girls and women in your world, and normalize those allyship relationships and discussions. Be intentional in raising a future male he-for-she ally.

INTERACTIONS WITH EXTENDED FAMILY OR THE GREATER COMMUNITY

Around Valentine's Day, a friend with a first grader shared that she bought cute rainbow valentines for her daughter to distribute to her classmates. The daughter asked, "Oh, can we get less girly ones for the boys?" Her mom said no, surprised by how much the innocent question bothered her. I don't blame this mom for her response, as this scenario shows how gender roles and patriarchal ideas surround us and can be evident even in these early years.

A mom of a grade schooler whom I spoke with noted that a coaching program at her workplace taught her about emotional intelligence, asking questions such as "How does this make the other person feel?" She felt the program was good for her work but even more informative at her home and in her parenting. As parents, we are the CEOs of our households, so it makes sense that these same emotional intelligence principles would come in handy for raising our kids. If something happens at school and your son is wondering why someone was upset about a situation, it's helpful to ask your son as a thought experiment to swap roles, metaphorically turn the situation around, and consider *others'* feelings. Baby steps in grade school serve as lessons that will stick with your son as he grows.

As your son's world expands, there will be highs and lows. Realize that there are valuable life lessons in the disappointments. Don't just sweep the inevitable negative experiences under the rug; these are important

THE FAMILY JOURNEY

Bumper Sticker Motto

The Golden Rule is a great rule for all of us to live by, whether we are a boy in grade school or an adult: Treat others the way you wish to be treated. Repeat this phrase often over the years; it's a great reminder for all of us.

moments in which your son will develop *resilience*. Being told no is OK, and the world will continue to rotate. Our sons need to know that boundaries are OK and that they can say no—and that there will also be times when others say no to them. Better yet, model this resilience in your own daily life. We as adults experience plenty of foibles and struggles, and these are opportunities to share with our sons to normalize resilience and adaptability: "I wanted X, but I got Y, so here's my new plan."

A parent of a fourth grader told me how her outer space–loving son eagerly applied to a Mars exploration program that he learned about at school. He put a lot of effort into his application, but unfortunately, he didn't get accepted. Although of course he and his family were disappointed, his parents made a point to applaud their son's effort, not the outcome. Also important, his parents encouraged him to congratulate the students who *were* chosen. Empathy, vulnerability. These boys are our future men, and they will make the world a better place.

THE CONCEPT OF CONSENT

The concept of *consent,* and the forms consent can take, continues to be important to raise our sons to be better men. When we tell our girls to not dress a certain way because it can tempt boys, it sends a message to boys *and* girls that boys have no control over themselves. The narrative needs to shift. Let's remind our sons that female bodies deserve to be respected and are not to be objectified, no matter how girls and women are dressed.

The school-age years are when your son will really start to notice differences between the culture of your household and that of his peers' households and of the world around him. Many of his friends and peers will have a positive impact. Conversely, he will also observe situations that perpetuate the patriarchy within families or communities. Whether it's regarding gender-equity ideas in particular or the world in general, your son will point out these differences. As a parent I found it helpful to say "Well, in *our* family…" followed by whichever philosophy we were working to adhere to. There's a way to respectfully discuss differences and diversity. In fact, it's helpful for your son to observe the range of perspectives, as well as play a role in how your family makes decisions and interacts with others.

Your son will develop friendships with kids of different genders. This is healthy. Avoid the temptation to label a close friend who happens to be a girl as a "girlfriend." Platonic friendship strengthens self-esteem and bully proofs a child. Additionally, your son may become close with kids whose parents have different viewpoints from yours. Use these situations as teachable moments, realize that the child is innocent from their parents' views, and consider the fact that you have an influence on that child's life experience as well.

TEACHABLE MOMENTS

Consume Media Together

The American Academy of Pediatrics recommends daily media limits for all ages, not only in duration of time but also in quality of programming. Think of media use as part of a varied diet. We cannot live on protein alone; we also need vegetables and other nutrients. Similarly, school-aged kids should engage in a variety of activities each day, including reading, going to school, and learning; playing; being physically active; and having conversations. Also in this equation is proper sleep, which can range from 8 to 12 hours a night, depending on your child's age. Media-free times (eg, mealtimes) and media-free zones (eg, your son's bedroom) are a great idea. School-aged children should not sleep with devices in their bedrooms; pediatricians strongly discourage televisions, computers, and smartphones in the bedroom.

On the subject of media consumption, Peggy Orenstein writes in her book *Boys & Sex:*

> [U]nchecked, media consumption of *any* kind is associated with greater tolerance for sexual harassment, belief in rape myths, early sexual initiation, sexual risk-taking, a greater number of partners, and stereotyping of women. Boys, too, then, need a strong counternarrative to develop grounded, realistic perspectives on women, men, sex, and love. Frankly,

without it, there is a chance that they won't see women as fully human, and that they will view sex as something a female partner does *for* them and that they do *to* her. Start young, by offering little boy's books, films, and other media featuring complex female protagonists.[8]

We'd be living in denial if we pretended it was easy to limit screens at this age, especially in a post-pandemic world. Enter the benefits of shared media use with your son: you can flip the script on media use by co-viewing media with your kids or even co-playing along with their preferred video game of the moment. What programs are your kids currently interested in? Make it a special event—you can even picnic on your family room floor, with a spread-out blanket on the floor, as well as special once-in-a-while snacks—and watch together. Let your son teach you how to play his favorite game of the moment. It's a natural self-esteem booster for your son to share what he's good at and passionate about with you.

In a balanced manner, ensuring that you don't overtake the experience with too much conversation, ask your son questions about the images you see when you watch media together. Often we discuss frequently overused stereotypes for girls, but there are male stereotypes as well that promote a limited view of masculinity and should be pointed out as such. "We always say this for girls, it's becoming somewhat commonplace with girls: 'Let's break apart the media. Let's poke the holes. Let's say princesses aren't real,'" Katie Hurley, child psychotherapist and author, has said. "But we have to do it with boys too, because you see these male advertisements for power protein things and these impossibly muscled enormous men with no shirts on, and we have to see that for boys, too. We have to give them the same opportunity to say, 'hey, this is not what every man in the world looks like.'"[9] The school-age years are a time when kids assign certain psychological characteristics to people with certain genders (eg, girls are more affectionate and emotional, boys are more aggressive and ambitious).[10] Point out the media you're watching and contrast it with real-world examples of fully fleshed-out individuals so your kids become more discerning in what they're watching. Many families choose to repeat a motto of "There are no boys or girls, only people." If you encounter

---

8. Orenstein P. *Boys & Sex: Young Men on Hookups, Love, Porn, Consent, and Navigating the New Masculinity*. Harper; 2020.
9. Wallace K. How to teach children about gender equality. CNN Health. October 2, 2017. Accessed May 17, 2023. https://www.cnn.com/2017/09/26/health/gender-equality-teaching-children-parenting/index.html.
10. Ward LM, Aubrey JS. *Watching Gender: How Stereotypes in Movies and on TV Impact Kids' Development*. Common Sense Media; 2017.

images that don't align with your greater gender-equity goals, use these as teachable moments to have a conversation about the issue.

Common Sense Media (www.commonsensemedia.org), introduced in Chapter 4, Nurturing Toddlers and Preschoolers to Be Better Men, continues to serve as a valuable media resource as your son grows. Common Sense Media media reviews not only inform parents if television shows, movies, video games, and more contain age-inappropriate (sexual, violent) content but also examine media for gender stereotypes and representation of a diverse array of people. Co-viewing media with your son means that even a scene that causes you to cringe can lead to conversations and teachable moments that help your son put fictional scenarios into the context of our IRL, in real life, worlds.

THE FAMILY JOURNEY

Common Sense Media Age-Appropriate Guidelines

What school-aged kids learn about gender

- They draw psychological distinctions between girls/women and boys/men (eg, girls are more emotional/affectionate, boys are more ambitious/aggressive).
- They learn associations of occupations and academic subjects with people of each gender.
- Their own gender stereotyping becomes more flexible.
- Their gender segregation strengthens.

Common Sense Media goals for media content

- Show role models who participate in both feminine and masculine behaviors and roles without ridicule from other characters, especially boys.
- Show role models who are focused on doing things, and who display emotions and sensitivity, based on context rather than gender.
- Show adults in traditional and nontraditional occupations, including women as professionals and men as caregivers.
- Show nonsexualized female characters and nonaggressive male characters who resolve conflict without resorting to violence.

Adapted from Ward LM, Aubrey JS. *Watching Gender: How Stereotypes in Movies and on TV Impact Kids' Development.* Common Sense Media; 2017.

Media has the power to expand or limit how our future men view themselves and the world around them. If we limit who and what our sons can be, we put our sons themselves at risk.

THE FAMILY JOURNEY

Hidden Speed Traps

If your son is a gamer, video gaming with your son promotes bonding, gives you insight into your son's world and interests, and allows him to teach you new skills, giving him a sense of mastery. An additional benefit: at the time you deem it appropriate to allow your son to partake in online video gaming, you can take an insider look at the communities with which he is communicating. Internet safety awareness is a moving target, as platforms evolve and change faster than your son's development. I've spoken with patients' families for whom even an 8-year-old boy can observe the influence of online gamers. Often gamer influencers share misogynistic or even counterculture views. Be aware of potential influencers by maintaining a presence in your son's online world, should you choose to allow him access.

Age-Appropriate Books and Media

First, a note about co-viewing films with your son: Do you know about the Bechdel Test? Created by Alison Bechdel, there are 3 key questions to consider when watching a movie.

1. Does the movie have at least 2 women?
2. Do the women talk with each other?
3. Do the women talk with each other about something other than a man?

You'll be shocked, especially when reviewing old favorites from the '80s or '90s, that many older films do not age very well.

Suggested Books to Read and Films to Discuss With Your Grade School Son

Ages 4 to 8 years

- Beaty A. *Ada Twist, Scientist*. Abrams Books for Young Readers; 2016.
- Bell K, Hart B. *The World Needs More Purple People*. Random House Children's Books; 2020. This book is about embracing the things that bring us together as humans: asking questions, laughing, using our voices (eg, singing, giving ideas, sharing opinions), and working hard (eg, fixing something that needs fixing, helping someone). Being purple has nothing to do with what you look like.
- Blackwood M. *Derek, the Knitting Dinosaur*. Lerner Publishing Group; 1990.
- Bradley KB. *Ballerino Nate*. Dial Press; 2006.
- Brown M. *Marisol McDonald Doesn't Match*. Children's Book Press; 2011. Others consider Marisol a mismatch of features that don't make sense. She has red hair and brown skin, likes to wear polka dot and stripe combinations, and eats peanut butter and jelly burritos. One day, she tries to "match" and please everyone and realizes that this doesn't make her happy. She's happy the way she is.
- Cole B. *Prince Cinders*. Putnam; 1997.
- Corey S. *You Forgot Your Skirt, Amelia Bloomer*. Scholastic Press; 2000.
- Gravel E. *The Cranky Ballerina*. HarperCollins Publishers; 2016. Ada does not like ballet and it makes her cranky. She discovers that it's not her thing, but perhaps karate is.
- Pearlman R. *Pink Is for Boys*. Running Press Kids; 2018.
- Rusch E. *For the Love of Music: The Remarkable Story of Maria Anna Mozart*. Tricycle Press; 2011.
- Shetterly ML. *Hidden Figures: The True Story of Four Black Women and the Space Race*. Harper; 2018.
- Stone TL. *Who Says Women Can't Be Doctors? The Story of Elizabeth Blackwell*. Henry Halt & Co; 2013.
- Toht P. *Dress Like a Girl*. Harper; 2019. Girls can wear whatever outfit makes them feel best.
- Yolen J, Stemple HEY. *Not All Princesses Dress in Pink*. Simon & Schuster Books for Young Readers; 2010. Princesses kick dirt, play soccer, wear stinky socks, wear jerseys, and use power tools.
- Zolotow C. *William's Doll*. HarperCollins Publishers; 1972.

Ages 5 to 10 years

- Levy D. *I Dissent: Ruth Bader Ginsburg Makes Her Mark*. Simon & Schuster Books for Young Readers; 2016. "Fight for the things that you care about. But do it in a way that will lead others to join you." —RBG. When Ruth was growing up in Brooklyn, NY, in the 1940s, despite it being a cultural melting pot with immigrants from all over the world, "[b]oys were expected to grow up, go out in the world, and do big things. Girls? Girls were expected to find husbands." But Ruth's mom thankfully disagreed.
- Mosca JF. *The Doctor With an Eye for Eyes; The Story of Dr. Patricia Bath*. Innovation Press; 2017.
- Whelan G. *The Boy Who Wanted to Cook*. Sleeping Bear Press; 2011.

Ages 9 to 12 years

- Holmes M, Hutchison T, Lowe K. *You-ology: A Puberty Guide for EVERY Body*. American Academy of Pediatrics; 2022. The most inclusive book about puberty to date, this book recognizes that separating boys and girls is an antiquated idea when it comes to puberty education. Respectful of the gender spectrum, nonbinary kids, and transgender kids, the authors recognize the need to educate everybody on what changes occur for all, promoting better understanding, communication, and empathy moving forward. A pioneering study by the Williams Institute, the first broad-based population estimate of its kind, showed that there are 1.2 million nonbinary LGBTQ+ adults in the United States.[11]
- Mosca JF. *The Girl With a Mind for Math; The Story of Raye Montague*. Innovation Press; 2018. An engineer in the 1970s took an alternative route because colleges in the 1950s did not allow Black students into their engineering programs.
- Riordan R. *The Lightning Thief*. Puffin Books; 2006. Percy Jackson and the Olympians. Although the main character is a boy, the brilliant Annabeth Chase, the daughter of the Greek goddess Athena, plays a main role.
- Shetterly ML. *Hidden Figures: Young Readers' Edition*. Harper; 2016.

(continued on next page)

---

11. Anders C. More than 1 million nonbinary adults live in the U.S., a pioneering study finds. *Washington Post*. June 22, 2021. Accessed May 26, 2023. https://www.washingtonpost.com/dc-md-va/2021/06/22/first-population-estimate-lgbtq-non-binary-adults-us-is-out-heres-why-that-matters.

Films

- *Coco*. Pixar Animation Studios; 2017. Although the main character is a 12-year-old boy, his tender relationship with Mama Coco illustrates the breadth and complexity that boys are capable of. Mama Coco, Mama Imelda, and Abuelita are 3 strong women who play important female characters and represent the significance of matriarchs in Latin culture.
- *Encanto*. Walt Disney Animation Studios; 2021. A female lead whose main character struggle is *not* about her relationship with a male character. How refreshing! The Madrigal clan's family matriarch, Abuela Alma, is a complex, textured character as well.

WORDS MATTER: PHRASES AT STAGES THAT DO US NO FAVORS

Perception becomes reality. The words we use hold great power. Each time we tell a young boy to "Man up" or "Toughen up," we are conveying a powerful message that our sons should swallow their feelings and forge ahead. As we continue to discover, encouraging our sons to bury their feelings means the anger or frustration or sadness will be released in other ways. Instead of telling young boys to "Put up or shut up," let's coach our sons to deal with their feelings in more constructive ways, whether through communication, exercise, redirection, or other methods.

Similarly, let's abolish the phrase that anyone does anything "like a girl": throwing, running, catching a ball, whatever. The inherent message here is that to exhibit a characteristic considered female is negative and undesirable.

When we tell our sons to "Be a man" or that "Real men don't cry," we teach boys to repress their feelings. We need to do better; we need to create safe spaces for our sons to express their emotions without fear of facing repercussion or ridicule.

Gay is another word still used on grade school playgrounds that can cause great harm. Teach your son that insulting someone or something as

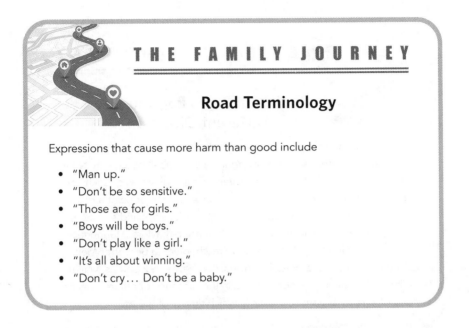

THE FAMILY JOURNEY

Road Terminology

Expressions that cause more harm than good include

- "Man up."
- "Don't be so sensitive."
- "Those are for girls."
- "Boys will be boys."
- "Don't play like a girl."
- "It's all about winning."
- "Don't cry... Don't be a baby."

"gay" is not acceptable. We need to educate our kids about LGBTQ+ people and their lives and the appropriate terminology. Talking with your children about LGBTQ+ communities will help them understand the context and significance of such insults. Make the conversation open and honest; by doing so, you will help reduce prejudice. Your kids should know they can always come and talk with you. When we teach our kids that there are many ways to be a man, we show them that gay can simply be how a person is.[12]

Informing others of our personal pronouns (for me, *she/her/hers*) is an inclusive choice to normalize the range of gender diversity. I recently came across a person bragging online that they "judge" people who use pronouns, finding the process silly. We use personal pronouns to express and normalize the range of gender identity; people who are nonbinary, gender fluid, gender nonconforming, or more should not feel ignored, shamed, or driven to depression.

---

12. Jones A. 9 ways to raise your son without toxic masculinity. Romper. February 14, 2017. Accessed May 17, 2023. https://www.romper.com/p/9-ways-to-raise-your-son-without-toxic-masculinity-37717.

THE FAMILY JOURNEY

When Signs Point in a Different Direction

There will be adults in your son's world who will use gendered or sexist language, or model bad behavior. Your son's baseball coach may tell a child to not "throw like a girl," or a grandparent will want to teach your son how to throw a football when your son would rather paint a picture or bake bread. Depending on the person, relationship, and situation, you may decide to "call in" or "call out" these behaviors. Mentioned in Chapter 4, Nurturing Toddlers and Preschoolers to Be Better Men, calling in means a one-on-one conversation between 2 parties, while calling out, done in the moment and in the presence of others, may be needed in more urgent scenarios in which time is of the essence.

Similarly, there are some antiquated titles that may be passé. Most men can be referred to as *Mr;* women, on the other hand, may be titled as *Miss, Ms,* or *Mrs.* In February 2022, a tweet[13] went viral: "My [8-year-old] with the worksheet mic drop. #thekidsarealright" accompanied by a school worksheet with 3 images of women asking whether they are Miss, Ms, or Mrs, and the boy answered, "I think she is a Dr." Great thinking, young man!

The aforementioned tweet reminded me of the old riddle, which only stumps people who don't yet realize that women can be physicians and surgeons: "A father and his son are in a car accident. The father dies at the scene and the son is rushed to the hospital. At the hospital, the surgeon looks at the boy and says, 'I can't operate on this boy, as he is my son.' How can this be? Answer: The surgeon is the mother of the patient."

Baseball practice, playdates, and multiplication tables will quickly evolve into the murky terrain of tweens and teens, middle school, and questions of smartphone readiness, among countless other new situations. In middle

---

13. @StephptaylorCLT. My 8 yo with the worksheet mic drop. #thekidsarealright. Accessed May 17, 2023. https://twitter.com/StephptaylorCLT/status/1494764017805676546.

school, our sons will receive yet more messages from peers, the media, and society to "be a man" with attempts to harden outer tough shells. Do you have to have a tough outer shell to be a man? We parents should watch for learning opportunities and scenarios to support our sons and nurture them as full humans, capable of connection, emotion, and nurturing.

RECOMMENDED RESOURCE FOR PARENTS OF SCHOOL-AGED BOYS

Lythcott-Haims J. *How to Raise an Adult: Break Free of the Overparenting Trap and Prepare Your Kid for Success.* St Martin's Press; 2015

Chapter 6

Nurturing Middle School Boys to Be Better Men: Promoting Equity Through a Time of Great Transition

The Lone Ranger, a fictional icon of American culture known for being an independent maverick, made his debut on radio in the 1930s, television in the 1950s, and has appeared in countless books. Generations have glorified the idea of a solitary figure fighting single-handedly for justice. Our society has idealized the idea of a man who works alone, who doesn't need the help of others. Yet is being alone good for people's mental health? Research tells us that social connections help bolster our emotional well-being. Our middle school sons' expanding social circles are an opportunity for them to connect with others, which can serve as a buffer of resilience when life gets tough. Perhaps we as a culture can do better to promote emotional connection rather than tell our sons they cannot rely on the support of others.

For generations, boys and men have often been the recipients of a loud and clear message: you need to fix this, and you need to do it alone, by yourself. As the mom of 3 young adult boys, I want my sons to feel connected to others, to feel safe being vulnerable with loved ones, and to know that if they need help, it is OK to reach out to others without fear of being shamed. Taking a broader look, one need only catch up on recent news events to know what happens when male figures, disconnected from others, choose to act out, with the most disastrous scenarios ending with violence. The reality is that overwhelmingly, school and mass shootings are carried out by male perpetrators. Our sons *need* support, connection, and community.

Over time, media has evolved from the traditional, often-used trope of the lone wolf, to introduce more modern male figures who aren't afraid to accept the help of others in their quests. A whole other discussion point is the relative paucity of films that feature complex female characters as the lead protagonist (the Bechdel Test works here: Are there 2 female characters who speak with each other about something other than a man?).

Although many films feature a male protagonist who swoops in, single-handedly saves the day, and rides off into the sunset, it's refreshing that *The Lightning Thief* fictional book series uses themes of connection, friendship, chosen family, and community. The initial books in the series take place during what would be Percy Jackson's middle school years. Percy could not have faced and overcome his hurdles without trusted friends and confidants Annabeth Chase and Grover at his side. The message here? You *don't* need to go it alone. We are here for you. Teamwork. Friendship. Vulnerability. Our sons should be able to share their struggles and allow the space for others to support them to play a role in the story. Juxtapose these scenarios with media figures such as Dirty Harry or Han Solo of Star Wars (*solo* is literally his name). More recently, the character Din Djarin as The Mandalorian in his eponymous Star Wars series, which intentionally echoes a lone cowboy, has a series of adventures that ultimately help him learn to accept the help from others. In one particular action sequence, he tells The Force–gifted The Child (Grogu, also known as Baby Yoda) to step aside and stay out of the fray. Djarin sees himself as a protector who must keep The Child safe at all costs; however, he will learn that The Child can actually help and stem the tide of events.

Why do we need to support and protect our middle school sons' emotional health? If we do not support our sons' mental health, their self-esteem suffers, and in some cases, tragedy can result. In February 2018, a teen boy opened fire with a semiautomatic rifle at his former high school in Parkland, FL, killing 17 people, mostly teenagers, and wounding 14 others. Dramatic scenario? Yes, and I intentionally use this to underscore the importance of communicating with our sons, allowing our sons to be whole people. There is a direct line between emotionally troubled boys and societal violence. Pediatricians' entire careers are focused on prevention. Just as we buckle our seat belts to prevent vehicle injuries, and just as we administer lifesaving vaccines to prevent infections and illness, we need to nurture and protect kids' mental health, not only because it's vital for the child themselves but also because it prevents mental health struggles and abuse of, and violence toward, others.

The week following the events in Parkland, as a response Michael Ian Black wrote about messaging to sons in a *New York Times* op-ed: "Too many boys are trapped in the same suffocating, outdated model of masculinity, where manhood is measured in strength, where there is no way to be vulnerable without being emasculated, where manliness is about having power over others."[1]

We need to allow our boys to fully express themselves, free of previous notions of gender limitations. Societal violence such as in Parkland are sad, extreme examples of how we can fail our sons. Daily actions to help our sons feel heard, to allow the space for our sons to express themselves, and to allow the freedom to pursue individual interests and hobbies yield a healthy basis for bolstering their self-esteem and resilience. An ounce of prevention is a pound of cure.

Black followed up the op-ed with a book, *A Better Man,* and on the subject of most school shootings being carried out by men, he wrote, "You can go through the list of mass shooters and you'll find the same thing in all of them: it's always somebody's son because it's always a boy."[2] As soon as I read this, I thought, "What a sobering thought. These mass shooters are *somebody's sons.*" As our babies turn to toddlers and our toddlers turn to little boys, we cherish every milestone and even every misstep as they learn to navigate the world around them. But when our boys turn to adolescents and, eventually, men, what potentially goes wrong? What steps can we take to help boys be their full human selves, help them develop their emotional intelligence, and help them use a robust vocabulary with which to define themselves?

Our boys and young men must be given safe spaces to express themselves. We need to normalize our tween son's ability to share his feelings, fears, and aspirations. In the younger toddler, preschool, and grade school years, our sons' feelings may be simpler for our families to navigate. By the tween and teen years, however, many of us parents may find ourselves perpetuating stereotypes carried through generations. If our seventh-grade son comes home from school and is upset about a situation with classmates,

---

1. Black MI. The boys are not all right. *New York Times.* February 21, 2018. Accessed May 17, 2023. https://www.nytimes.com/2018/02/21/opinion/boys-violence-shootings-guns.html.
2. Black MI. *A Better Man: A (Mostly Serious) Letter to My Son.* Algonquin Books of Chapel Hill; 2020.

or doesn't want to talk after an athletic event, decades of generational trends may cause us to shrug our shoulders and assume our sons are taking on that familiar, presumably "male" "I don't want to talk" mentality. And there will be times when it's perfectly appropriate to allow a situation to breathe before talking about it. The best communication involves knowing that there's an appropriate time, and place, for positive connection. Certainly, in the heat of the moment, when one or both parties are upset, there cannot be a meaningful communication or exchange of ideas. But silence, and shrugging of the shoulders, cannot be the only or final response by parents. How can we talk with our tween and teen sons when they don't want to talk?

DAILY INTERACTIONS PROVIDE COMMUNICATION OPPORTUNITIES

As adults ourselves, we have good days, bad days, and in-between days. Sometimes we will want to talk about them, and sometimes we won't. Do we afford our kids the same opportunity to choose *whether* and *how* they talk about their good and bad days? If your son does speak up about a particular challenge, you should provide support, pause to take in the information, and actively listen in a nonjudgmental manner. "I see," "That must have been frustrating," and "How are you feeling right now?" are all good statements and questions that will nudge the conversation forward. Allow for natural pauses, ebbs and flows, in the conversation; all too often, we adults try to steer the ship, to the detriment of the true exchange of thoughts, ideas, and feelings, causing our children to shut down emotionally. As parents, we want to make sure to listen more and to speak and guide less.

Frequently, we want to jump into a familiar, protective parent mode (years of practice of actively parenting younger children has instilled this within us) and begin to problem-solve for our kids. You may find yourself wanting to interrupt your tween son, suggesting solutions to modify and somehow remedy the situation. Just a decade ago, our sons were babies and their daily existence depended on our constant involvement and leadership. But we should remember that we have been teaching lessons to them all along. The fact is that we parents now need to shift gears and adopt a different style of communicating with our adolescents, a style that is engaged with more *listening* and less "I'll jump in and fix everything."

THE FAMILY JOURNEY

Turn Down the Volume to Better Read the Road

Parenthood is ever-changing. As soon as you've "figured out" the current stage, your child has moved on to a new phase. Now that your son is middle school age, your communication with each other will evolve. Learn to listen more than you talk, and get into the habit, when your son shares an issue with you, of asking him "Would you like me to just listen, or would you like my advice?"

For some parents, this can be a struggle. A good habit to get into is to ask your son "Do you want me to listen so you can vent, or do you want me to help brainstorm solutions?" This question serves 3 purposes. The first is that from a practical standpoint, your son gets to decide the tenor of the conversation. The second is that the question itself sets the greater stage and models healthy communication. A conversation can adopt different styles to suit different needs on different days. The question empowers your son to realize he can advocate for what kind of talk he has with others. After all, these conversations with our sons form the basis for how they'll interact with others around them for years to come. How refreshing to know that years from now, your son will be speaking with someone who had a bad day and, after years of modeling, will ask that other individual "Would you like me to just listen, or do you want my help in brainstorming solutions?" Modeling empathy is a great way to help our sons learn empathy. The third purpose of this question is that it puts your son in the driver's seat of the scenario. It is an antidote to helicopter (over-involved) parenting, which doesn't do our kids any favors. Your son is not a passive passenger on his journey; he can elicit input from loved ones, but ultimately, he should choose his next steps. These subtle ways of communicating will support your son as he grows into a better man, taking responsibility for his choices and actions.

THE FAMILY JOURNEY

Fellow Passengers Along for the Ride

Your middle school son's friend circle will include other genders and kids whose family values may not align with yours. Resist the temptation to label friendships with girls as romantic, and use differing values among friends' families as a conversation topic.

When my own kids were small, I read a wise piece of advice, and I really wish I remembered where I read it. I'll paraphrase it here: "By the time your kids reach the age of 12 years, they already know your opinion on everything under the sun. Now is the time when we parents need to stop talking so much and start *listening* to our child more." As a parent, you'll be amazed at the perspective and wisdom of your tween son. I've lost count of how many times I've learned a thing or two from the insights of Gen Z, whether it's my own kids or the patients I care for in my primary care pediatrics clinic. Conversing with our sons is so much more than exchanging information or teaching our kids how to do something. Talking with our middle school sons is an opportunity to set the stage for healthy communication, an open-ended back-and-forth that acknowledges the feelings of the other person and demonstrates empathy.

In earlier chapters, we discussed a conversation strategy of "highs and lows" or "apples and onions." I maintain that this is a great method to communicate with anyone of any age, even adults. Alternatively, there are plenty of card games available in which each card has a conversation starter for mealtime or any time. In my busy life as a working mom, I was never organized enough to use the card games, so I kept to the highs and lows. Simple can be best. Asking about the best and worst parts of the day can spark an entirely larger conversation. Both son and parent should participate; it's crucial that your son understands that *you* have daily struggles and inconveniences you work through as well. That's life after all. The actual best/worst part doesn't even matter; it's the fact that it will get you sharing feelings and developing empathy for each other.

There is value to sharing a space even if words aren't being exchanged. The occasional pause or silence allows the opportunity for spontaneous conversation to arise, made even better if the conversation is initiated by a son rather than the parent. Some of the best insights I've learned about my sons were from the little chats that occurred when we were simply together, working on a shared task, or were sharing space in the same part of the home. Be curious about your son's life. All too often, we adults focus on the "doing": grades, school, chores. Don't just ask your son whether he's done with his homework or whether he has brushed his teeth. Ask your son's opinion on music, games, and the rest of his life. Allow your relationship to breathe, avoid yes-or-no questions, and ask open-ended questions.

THE FAMILY JOURNEY

The Things You Learn Along the Way

Often your most meaningful chats with your son will happen organically, without a plan, while you are doing other things. Minimize distractions and put away screens to allow these moments to occur.

ROLE MODELING AS PARENTS

Chores are an increasingly important part of our sons' maturation process. In the tween years, our boys are becoming more involved in the greater community (eg, school, extracurricular activities including sports, youth clubs, religious education). Despite increasingly complex schedules, we need to remember that the basic parenting goal of teaching boys life skills also promotes gender equity. Additionally, participating and sharing in the household chores sets the stage for teamwork for years to come. If you find that your son's time is overscheduled with activities such as soccer or musical instrument practice and he doesn't "have time" to regularly take out the kitchen garbage (as one example), it's time to step back and consider the bigger picture. Perhaps the *schedule* itself is the problem. Work with your son to honestly evaluate weekly commitments and, if needed, eliminate the 1 or 2 least important elements of the schedule so he has the time and ability to develop as a full person. All too often, our tweens and teens are so overscheduled with activities that they're not learning the practical life skills of participating in the shared responsibility of maintaining a household.

At times, it can be cultural or generational family trends that stunt a boy's development as an active participant helping the household run smoothly. There are families for whom chores are considered "below" the male role within the household. As a parent, you yourself may be aware of the need for your son to develop life skills, but grandparents or other relatives may judge or vocally criticize the fact that you ask your son to help with necessary tasks. This can be especially challenging for multigenerational households. Stay strong, knowing that you are taking the right steps. Confidently make a statement about how it's important that your son regularly contribute to running the home, and know that this is a choice for you as a parent to make. Explain your rationale, that you are trying to teach your child about gender equity. Also, remember that our sons are watching and listening to these interactions, so overhearing you share these important philosophies with other family members can be even more powerful than simply talking about them together.

Combating cultural gender inequity to friends and family may not always be easy. Nigerian author Chimamanda Ngozi Adiche writes in her book *We Should All Be Feminists*:

> I know a family who has a son and a daughter, a year apart in age, both brilliant at school. When the boy is hungry, the parents say to the girl, "Go and cook Indomie noodles for your brother." The girl doesn't like to cook Indomie noodles, but she is a girl and she has to. What if the parents, from the beginning, taught *both* children to cook them? Cooking, by the way, is a useful and practical life skill for a boy to have. I've never thought it made much sense to leave such a crucial thing—the ability to nourish oneself—in the hands of others.[3]

Of course, both boys and girls should develop these important life skills. It's common sense, but sadly, common sense isn't always that common.

---

3. Adichie CN. *We Should All Be Feminists*. Vintage Books; 2012.

THE FAMILY JOURNEY

Maintenance to Keep the Journey Going

Our middle school sons are capable of all the tasks mentioned in previous, younger-themed chapters, and now that they are older and maturing, some ideas to add to your list are

- Doing their own laundry
- Helping prepare meals, preparing simple meals on their own
- Packing school lunch (the night before)
- Taking out garbage and recycling
- Cleaning their bedroom and other areas of the shared home
- Washing the car

As my sons grew into the middle school years, I worked to increase their involvement in our kitchen. More kid involvement in the kitchen can cut across your natural grain, especially if you're a particularly orderly and clean parent like me. Much like in the younger years, getting tweens involved in the kitchen absolutely creates more "work" and mess, but I cannot overemphasize the need to continue this learning process. Life's basic necessities include food and shelter, so yes, our sons need to learn about food prep. In the early years, I began to think of our kitchen as a science laboratory of sorts, a place for culinary journeys, exploring simple recipes, dishes, and "experiments." As our kids grew, so did the complexity of the science experiments. In the past, I myself have made years of awkward dishes that taught me how *not* to cook just as much as how *to* cook. Mistakes are part of the culinary learning process. Heck, one of the most beloved Persian dishes, the crispy rice of tahdig, translated to "bottom of the pot," was likely invented by accident because of a forgotten rice pot cooking over a stove!

Safety first, of course, and depending on your son's prior experience and level of maturity, sharp knives, hot stoves, and ovens should be used only with a trustworthy adult nearby. That said, it is time to loosen the reins a bit and let your son take the lead on cooking. Grilled cheese and scrambled eggs absolutely count. Many of us have a sweet tooth, so baking can be an entryway to kitchen familiarity that eventually translates to all sorts of future dishes, both sweet and savory. Use screens to your advantage here; there are countless online recipes meant for kids and tweens to cook that include helpful instructional videos. In my clinical pediatrics practice, I always joke with my tween patients about the myriad of kids' cooking television shows that feature 12-year-olds who seem to already be master chefs; if those kids can cook and bake, so can we.

By the time my sons hit their teen years, I instituted a new routine for summers and longer school vacations: each boy chose a night of the week to plan and cook dinner for the family. In the earlier years, they'd choose a recipe in advance (thanks to the internet, you'll never be lacking for recipes; even google the ingredients in your fridge right now and you'll get some great choices) and I would shop and make sure the ingredients were on hand ahead of time. As my sons got older and earned their drivers' licenses, the job evolved to include shopping for ingredients themselves and then making the meal, rounding out their executive planning skills. A bit of friendly advice: if the recipe says it takes "45 minutes" to make, *double* this prep time so you're not eating dinner at midnight. Just sayin'. A night of dinner prep taken off your plate (pun intended)? Check. Your son gaining

valuable life skills and the executive functioning skills of planning, understanding, and following instructions, including measuring ingredients? Check. Your family learning a new recipe that may not have already been in your meal rotation? Check. A self-esteem booster for your son to provide delicious nourishment for his family? Check. It's a win on all counts.

The COVID-19 pandemic gave an opportunity for more kids to become involved in the kitchen. We all spent more time preparing meals at home instead of taking meals in restaurants. Choose your food cravings and make those dishes yourselves at home. Also, as discussed in previous chapters, on birthdays, major holidays, and family events, involve your sons and make sure the planning, cooking, and cleanup tasks are shared equitably among people of all genders in the home.

THE FAMILY CALENDAR

In previous chapters, we discussed strategies to stem the tide of generations-old traditions of the female parent, often the mom, as the gatekeeper to all family logistics, planning, and general information. Teaching awareness of these habits, patterns, and trends, with conscious decisions to help your son make different choices, will create incremental changes to shift our families toward greater gender equity. For younger age-groups, we discussed strategies to keep all the adults on the same page. Now that your son has reached middle school age, it's time to start passing the baton to your son to take part in the family logistics, scheduling, and planning dynamic. Tell him to pick out a color marker that will represent him on

Our Family Calendar

Sunday	Monday	Tuesday	Wednesday	Thursday	Friday	Saturday
13	14	15	16	17	18	19
9:00 am religious education	Coding club after school	Dentist at 11:00 am— Dad will pick up/drop off	5:00 pm tae kwon do	Volunteer event 4:00–6:00 pm (Entire family)	5:00 pm Tae kwon do Grocery shopping	Grandpa's birthday—Dad will pick up cake

the family calendar. Celebrate his age and the expectations of him now that he is older. This should be an exciting, empowering step for him.

The tween years are an age-appropriate time to emphasize skills of all kinds, including advocating for oneself, honing executive functioning, and taking part in logistics and planning. As an example, at this age, if your tween gets invited to a birthday party, they should plot it on the calendar. If your son thinks a gift is going to magically appear for his friend's birthday, ask him how that is going to happen. Teach your son that the party is not just a date on the calendar. Your tween needs to learn that in addition to day-of logistics of a ride to the party and a pickup from the party, advance planning is needed to obtain a gift. The mental load is not just the responsibility of a parent, and it's definitely not just the responsibility of a mom. Dads, and now tween sons, can help distribute the mental load.

Our sons should take on increased responsibility for planning, especially as much more of their lives may now revolve around socializing with friends and participating in extracurriculars, religious education, or athletics. The details of dates on the calendar can be discussed on Sunday nights (or the family's chosen day and time) when the family together reviews the upcoming week's plan.

Use a giant paper calendar in a central part of your home (ours is in the kitchen; I've never used dry-erase boards because I've always worried about important events getting inadvertently erased; #LargeFamilyProblems). An added reason to use a large, physical family calendar is to limit screen

THE FAMILY JOURNEY

Another Pair of Eyes on the Road

As time moves on, the family calendar will continue to be a useful tool. During your tween son's middle school years, it will evolve as he plays a greater role in not just what happens when but additionally the logistics of the carpooling, who drives to which activities and who picks up, and any other advance planning required.

time as much as we can. Yes, smartphones are convenient, but I appreciate ways to help middle school kids look up important information in a method other than consulting a glowing screen that fits into the palms of their hands.

THE FAMILY JOURNEY

Planning the Route

An idea to help each family member stay organized and to prevent a parent, usually a mom, from being the gatekeeper of all information is to hold a family meeting on Sunday nights, or a day and time of your choosing. The agenda? Go over the upcoming week's events and note who has what going on, as well as the logistics required to make those events happen. This gives tweens practice with executive functioning skills, and it's healthy to learn what's happening in their parent's worlds as well.

Working schedules and a busy middle school schedule mean that carpooling will likely play a larger role in your weekly schedule; your son should take some ownership in communicating with his peers and teammates to be aware of who is picking up whom and when, without constant text reminders from a parent. How often do moms remind *everyone,* adults and kids alike, of the daily plan, including texting individuals or the group as certain times approach? Much of this communication is within reason, but if you are a mom, or have found yourself in the position of reminding, make sure you self-reflect, consider the big picture, and do not hold everyone's hands to the point that if your son doesn't get a reminder text from his mom, he has no idea what's going on.

Do you know about the term *learned incompetence*? It's when a child or an adult is coached or reminded to excess to the point that the individual does not develop (or begins to forget) basic executive functioning skills. At the time of this writing, a social media video went viral. It was meant to be adorable and loving; however, I found it rather concerning: a woman mapped out her male partner's entire grocery store trip. She didn't just hand him a list; she gave excruciatingly specific steps so he would have his hand virtually held for the entire excursion. This was an *adult* shopping, by the way. This is grocery shopping, not defusing a nuclear bomb. It may not seem like a big deal to overcoach our partner or our son when they embark on a task, but I'd advocate for taking the long view on these scenarios and preventing family habits that perpetuate learned incompetence. Our sons are future men, and baby steps today (and, occasionally, a missed carton of milk) lead to better life skills as time goes on.

THE FAMILY JOURNEY

Map Your Route

The family calendar is a powerful tool to help coach your son in life skills and executive functioning skills. Features include

- Each person is represented by a different color on the calendar.
- Each person is responsible for adding after-school activities, due dates for school projects, practices, doctor appointments, orthodontist appointments, and friends' birthday parties.

If your child has a cell phone, they can take a photo of the calendar each week as a reminder of the day's activities or they can use a shared calendar app with all the family members. Alternatively, kids can add their schedules in their homework notebook too.

SCHOOL COMMUNICATION

At the start of the academic year (or even the prior spring, when you register your son for the upcoming year), your son's school will ask for each student's emergency contact information, including a phone tree with the order of preference to notify family if your son comes down with a fever or vomits during school hours, for example. School staff will typically default to calling moms, so make sure you make intentional choices when specifying your family phone tree. If there are times a parent has a cannot-miss work event, make sure the other parent is on tap for school emergencies and is ready and able to respond to calls and notifications.

Many schools release the dates of special school events, holidays, and vacations on the district website the prior spring. Dads can and should find this information and add it to the family calendar; it's not just the job of moms. Families can find a way to sync the school calendar, as well as athletic events and other extracurriculars, to the family calendar. Our competitive swim team released an online calendar, and when my sons were in middle school, I had 4 different kids in 3 different practice groups that met at different times, often on different days and even in different pools located in different towns. Thank goodness we figured out a way for technology to sync the calendar to our smartphones so kids and parents alike could easily figure out when and where practice was after school. This information is not just for a female parent to wrangle; *everyone* has a responsibility to be in the know.

Also, in the spirit of ensuring that a single parent does not become the gatekeeper of all information, all adults and kids in the house should have access to the family calendar. Pay attention as time passes: if you are a mom, or have found yourself in the position of gatekeeping, and family members (tween son *or* dad) keep asking you for information that is easily found in the shared calendar, kindly direct them to the family calendar to figure out the issue on their own. Moms could spoon-feed the others information, sure; a better, more valuable solution is to help our sons and partners find the information themselves.

RESILIENCE, EXPLORING INTERESTS

Middle school is an opportunity for boys to spread their wings, try new things in a lower-stakes environment, expand their social circles, and even experiment with different personas. It's also a great trial period for your son to take more ownership over his choices and self-care. I'll never forget the wise words of my own kids' middle school principal on this subject. Each spring, she holds a parent night for incoming families. Having had 4 kids in 3 different grades, I've been fortunate to hear her set the stage for parents more than once. I'm also grateful because sometimes I needed her dose-of-reality reminder to keep the big picture in mind. To paraphrase Dr Groen, "No one, years from now, will ask to see your child's junior high transcript. *Let them fail.* Consider junior high a warm-up for the high school years. The lessons they learn in junior high will stay with them for years to come." I'll add that you can learn as much from your failures as your successes. We parents need to keep being reminded of this, right? How often do we find ourselves interfering too much in, micromanaging, and overscheduling our kids' lives to the point where we could do more harm than good?

Allowing our sons to be fully realized people promotes gender equity. Our sons, and our daughters, do not fit into pre-prescribed boxes. Realize that your son's interests may vary widely from yours. *That is OK.* Celebrate this and learn with your kid. You were an athlete growing up, but your son loves music or theater (or both)? Wonderful. Meet your kid where they are. You were an art prodigy to the point of incorporating art into your now-adult career? Beautiful, and it's OK that your son is instead obsessed with ice hockey. Expand your views on what your son can be interested in so that self-determination is a theme for your son. Open-ended possibility helps our sons be whole people and doesn't force them to fit into a narrow box. Gender equity respects all people as whole individuals and does not define them just on the basis of their sex assigned at birth.

It is not only OK for your son to have completely different interests than you do, past or present, but also an advantage because you're learning the world of his interest together; you're both novices as you go. How powerful for our kids to learn how a *growth mindset* (vs a fixed mindset) works and that we're never too old to learn new things. My kids' main sports while growing up were competitive swimming and distance running. I did neither of these growing up. I learned firsthand that there is a beauty in *not* knowing the mechanics or inner workings of your kids' activities inside out. It gives space for your son to *own* the activity himself, develop at his own pace, and take it to the level he himself desires. Whether he takes the activity casually or competitively, or when there's a particular skill he wants to hone or improve on, it's up to *him* to talk with his coaches, leaders, and instructors to make the necessary modifications. I remember sitting next to other swimming club parents during practice or meets and overhearing their critiques of their child's butterfly kick, for example. I never had this issue because I really couldn't tell you the particulars of a successful butterfly kick. Ignorance is bliss! It was a wonderful silver lining that my kids had a swimming-naive mom, and they could simply *own* the sport themselves. My job was to support my kids, drive them, feed them, and cheer them on; they weren't going to get any backstroke tips from me. And this is a *good* thing. Self-determination,

THE FAMILY JOURNEY

Watch the Signs

Talk with your son about what's happening in his world. You'll likely learn about a bullying incident that occurred at school or at an activity. Teach your son that if it is safe to do so, to call out peers who are being disrespectful to others or who are telling sexist jokes. It can be difficult to be the only peer in a group not laughing along, but if your son believes a joke to be inappropriate, help him understand he has the power to call out his peer on it, or, at a minimum, to ask the peer "What do you mean by that?" which can be a subtler way to give the peer a chance to dial back or modify their inappropriate joke.

and knowing that there is a range of possibilities, is a path to gender equity. Our sons, as well as our daughters, deserve the opportunity to decide their own paths and destinies.

In the next chapter, we'll discuss a phrase coined by author Don McPherson: "aspirational masculinity," which aims to broaden what a boy can aspire to be. In our efforts to combat toxic masculinity, all too often, gender conversations induce feelings of shame and guilt and emphasize the ideas of what boys *shouldn't* do rather than the range of possibility of what they *can do*. Let's allow boys to be full humans.

SEX EDUCATION AT HOME AND AT SCHOOL

Sex education ranks as one of the more stressful topics that parents are hesitant to discuss with kids, yet having these conversations, early and often, is so important. The old-school notion of a single, mega conversation about the birds and the bees is outdated. We now know that sex education occurs over years, in an age-appropriate, stepwise manner, and consists of a series of mini conversations as your kids grow and develop. As scenarios pop up in real life and in the media, our kids will ask us questions and these can serve as inspirations for impromptu mini chats. Often, we adults attribute way more significance and meaning to these heady topics that may or may not be age appropriate for our kids. If as a parent, you're caught off guard by such a question, you can buy some time, formulate your own thoughts, and, most importantly, gauge your child's level of understanding by asking "What do *you* think?" A brief conversation followed by moving on with your day is a common way for this scenario to unfold.

Having an open-door policy for sex-related questions and conversations becomes even more vital as our sons are of middle school age. In fact, our idea of what constitutes "sex ed" is often overly restrictive. We should teach kids about sexuality, our bodies, our development, our boundaries, consent, what happens to boys and girls during pubertal development, and so much more. If you've established a pattern of nonjudgmental, open conversation with your son on a variety of topics, it will pay dividends as your son begins puberty and his social circles become more complex.

It's a missed opportunity to leave sex ed "to the school" for many reasons. If you're hesitant to discuss sex topics with your son, you should understand that the void *will* be filled by media, peers, and the world around him. With you as a parent, your child deserves the opportunity to discuss and explore these issues in a safe, nonjudgmental, supportive space. If not with you, then who?

Parents should not assume that "someone else" will teach tweens about sex ed. Our definitions of what sex ed should be, versus what it has actually become, continue to evolve over the decades, and according to adolescent experts, the version as it appears in our schools is surprisingly becoming more limited in scope as time goes on. Ideally, appropriate sex ed can

THE FAMILY JOURNEY

Navigating a Challenging Road

Both dads and moms can and should talk with tween sons about sex education topics. In past years, "The Talk" was often tasked to the parent of the same gender. Many smaller conversations from both parents, if possible, are preferable to expand your son's perspective on issues.

reduce unintended pregnancy, sexually transmitted infections, bullying, and sexual abuse, and it can enhance tweens' and teens' understanding of and ability to consent to sex. Is this what our kids are learning, however? The *Journal of Adolescent Health* published a study that examined national sex ed trends from 2011 to 2019, and it noted that despite national guidelines, including the Surgeon General Healthy People 2030 initiative highlighting the objective of sex ed, including formal instruction on delayed sex, birth control methods, HIV/AIDS prevention, and sexually transmitted infections, there is great discrepancy between individual states, as well as further variation at both district and school levels. A study by Laura Lindberg, PhD, and Leslie Kantor, PhD, highlighted concerning inequities in sex ed that can leave adolescents vulnerable to health problems and can prohibit their access to accurate and timely information.[4]

As our teens move through adolescence, all too often, their first sexual encounters have occurred before they even receive information about how to say no to sex, how to read a partner's cues, how to understand consent, where to get birth control, how to use a condom, and much more. The Society for Adolescent Health and Medicine has been outspoken in what they call a "crisis in sex education" and have brought attention to sex ed curricula that omits topics and focuses on marriage and abstinence. According to the Columbia University Mailman School of Public Health:

> [C]omprehensive sex ed curricula provide adolescents with accurate information, opportunities to explore their identities and values, and skillsets in communication and decision-making…, [endorsing] clear, age-appropriate instruction to reduce risk behaviors among adolescents and improve their overall health and wellbeing.…
>
> "[S]exual orientation and gender identity [as well as social determinants of health, disabilities, reproductive justice, PrEP therapy for HIV infection, and adolescent rights and minor consent laws] are foundational to any sex education program," said David Bell, MD, MPH…. "Adolescents need clear guidance to explore these topics both in the exploration of their own identities and to be able to navigate the world around them."[5]

---

4. Lindberg L, Kantor L. Adolescents' receipt of sex education in a nationally representative sample, 2011–2019. *J Adolesc Health*. 2021;70(2):290–297.
5. Irving Medical Center. Adolescent health professionals critique new abstinence-only sex ed standards. October 21, 2021. Accessed May 17, 2023. https://www.publichealth.columbia.edu/public-health-now/news/adolescent-health-professionals-critique-new-abstinence-only-sex-ed-standards.

Parents should be aware of the fact that sex ed programs at school can be limited and should take necessary action to make sure their son still has access to important information.

Parents who seek to empower boys and girls more equitably need to have more conversations with their tween sons, no matter how uneasy that makes parents feel or how embarrassed that makes our sons feel because the conversation is "cringe." If you're feeling awkward, it's OK to diffuse the situation with humor. Better to laugh and educate than to remain silent and let the internet and media fill the void.

THE FAMILY JOURNEY

Ensuring the Correct Path

When discussing the concept of consent with your son, a key element is that only an enthusiastic yes, when intimate, is actual consent. Additionally, consent can be withdrawn at any time. Dads and moms may feel that it's too early for these conversations, and tweens may consider the conversations cringeworthy; however, it's better to have a talk about it before your son experiences the situation—and our sons listen to us more than we think.

Pediatrician Kathryn Lowe, MD, FAAP, stated in an NPR interview about her book *You-ology,* coauthored with Melisa Holmes, MD, FACOG, and Trish Hutchison, MD, FAAP:

> There's a real need for all kids to understand about periods and erections, so we all understand each other's bodies. That really sets the stage for healthy communication and intimate relationships, if they so choose, growing up.
>
> I think the other big need is kids who don't fit into a gender binary. With this book, we're trying to change that language to be more inclusive. With traditional puberty education, whether it's in schools or in books, we talk about how girls get their periods and boys get erections. But some girls—for example, transgender girls—might not get their periods. They need to understand about erections and those changes in their bodies.

Regarding teaching puberty in a way that respects gender diversity, the authors explained, "There's lots of different ways you can use language to be more inclusive than traditional language when it comes to talking about puberty.... 'for most girls, this happens; for most boys, this happens.'"[6] Readers, your own introduction to sex ed was probably lacking. We've learned a lot with time. When having ongoing conversations with your tween son, do not shy away from topics such as erections, gender identity, and the fact that we are all unique.

To develop empathy, we must continue to work to put ourselves in others' shoes. Certain issues that are typical for a portion of the general population need to be normalized. As just one example, tween boys can learn to not consider aspects of menstruation "weird," "gross," or "taboo." The monthly menstrual cycle is just one example of a regular, healthy occurrence that still seems off-limits to speak of in some circles. For how many years have those of us who menstruate gasped with embarrassment when a hygiene pad or tampon fell out of our bag? All too often, our monthly menstrual periods have been cause for embarrassment or shame, yet it's all a typical part of being a person who menstruates. Some schools have begun to offer free sanitary supplies in school restrooms, but society still promotes a stigma for menstrual periods. No boy, whether or not he lives in a household with a sister, mom, or family member who has periods, should be aghast at the sight of a sanitary napkin or tampon. Period pain, smells, menstrual products, and clotting are all typical, so the fact that they exist shouldn't be hidden. If no one with periods lives in a home, it will be a greater challenge (and will probably bring you some eye rolls) to randomly bring up this topic (appropriate books and media can help), yet it's an important topic to bring up and discuss frequently enough to normalize it.

ON WHY PORNOGRAPHY IS INAPPROPRIATE: CONVERSATIONS BETWEEN PARENTS AND SONS

Regardless of parental controls, kids will often find ways to access pornography, referred to as *porn* for short. It's disheartening how easy it is to unintentionally stumble on porn even if you aren't seeking it out. Add the ubiquitous nature of screens and it's a game of Whac-A-Mole for a parent to try to limit a kid's access. It is of vital importance for parents to discuss with tween sons

---

6. Huang P. A new puberty guide for kids aims to replace anxiety with self-confidence. Shots: Health News From NPR. April 23, 2022. Accessed May 17 , 2023. https://www.npr.org/sections/health-shots/2022/04/23/1094260259/a-new-puberty-guide-for-kids-aims-to-replace-anxiety-with-self-confidence.

why porn is inappropriate. Porn perpetuates false notions of "normal" sexual partner behavior and perpetuates misogyny and the treatment of women as objects to be used simply for the pleasure of men. Grown-ups have an important opportunity to explain why porn is not healthful material with which to engage. The images that kids can come across can be very confusing and can make them feel uncomfortable. Having these conversations before that happens can help normalize it for your kids. And allow them to come talk with you. It's not a matter of if your child will come across these images but when. So, prepare your son with the knowledge to better handle it.

THE FAMILY JOURNEY

Open Your Eyes

Years in clinical pediatrics practice have informed me that most parents don't even want to think about their tween son and *puberty,* let alone the existence of pornography and the potential impact that it can have on their son. Sadly, porn is ubiquitous and a child's first encounter with porn is often unintentional, following an innocent internet search. Parents have an important voice to educate our sons, our future men, about how porn can distort their view of women, as well as their future relationships.

Paul Wright, PhD, associate professor of media at Indiana University who conducts research on how porn viewing affects male and female views of intimate relations, hypothesizes an association between age of first porn use and expressions of sexual dominance. Peggy Orenstein describes in her 2020 book, *Boys & Sex,* associations between "porn consumption and men's desire to engage in a range of aggressive behaviors, especially if the men drank regularly before sex."[7] Orenstein's interviews with more than 100 boys and young men ranging in age from 16 to 22 years revealed that they "believed porn had been damaging in ways that no adult had ever

---

7. Orenstein P. *Boys & Sex: Young Men on Hookups, Love, Porn, Consent, and Navigating the New Masculinity.* Harper; 2020.

discussed with them, and that they had never previously discussed with an adult." The message is loud and clear: as uncomfortable as it is, we need to discuss porn with our kids and put it into appropriate context.

SEXTING AND THE CONCEPT OF CONSENT

Ubiquitous screens mean that for current middle schoolers, texting and social media apps are a primary source of communication. Sexting, the sharing of intimate photos or messages, can be solicited or unsolicited. One important thing for anyone to consider is that "If you don't want someone to stand up in the crowded lunch cafeteria at school reading (or showing) the text, don't send it." Alternatively, if you wouldn't show your grandmother the text or message, don't send it. Middle school kids, developmentally, often feel infallible, and their decision-making still has years to mature. Too many scenarios of kids sending inappropriate images (nudes, as one example), requesting such images from a boy or a girl with whom they are texting, and sharing these images with others abound. Open, honest conversations with your kid, emphasizing boundaries, consent, and empathy, are key.

The concept of consent continues to evolve. Many of us, men and women alike, grew up learning that no means no, but a growing belief is that consent should also be affirmative: yes means yes. Continue the ongoing conversations with your kids about consent. Ideally, the foundation was set in earlier years, on which more layers can be built, but if not, it's never too late to begin these vital conversations.

The notion that boys are the ones who are always "pushing for more" is not the whole story; we need to remember that boys, like girls, can be subjected to unwanted advances, sexual harassment, or assault. In 2021, a male professional sports player came forward as having survived sexual assault by a coach in 2010. The team was made aware of the assault at the time, but it took no action on this information, placing other individuals at risk for abuse. I mention this scenario because all too often, abuse can and does happen everywhere. We all need to keep our eyes open and educate our sons. Burying our heads in the sand to avoid the unpleasant reality of sexual abuse does nothing to help would-be victims. If abuse can occur in a professional sports organization, believe me, it can occur anywhere, despite our shock each and every time we learn of a new scenario.

Sadly, subsequent events underscore how far we have yet to come in dealing with gendered abuse cases, preventing victim blaming, and creating a space in which individuals who have experienced harassment or abuse will feel comfortable with coming forward. After the above events, when asked about it by a reporter, the team owner replied, "It's time to move on." I'm an avid sports fan, and when I was listening to radio coverage the morning after the team owner's comment, a caller wisely pointed out what a *privilege* it is for the team owner to forget and move on, as those who have experienced sexual assault cannot simply "move on" themselves. This excellent point was followed by 2 unfortunate comments by other callers. One blatantly stated, "(The victim) is a grown man... Get over it." A different caller said, "I just want to be entertained; why does this have to be political?" These old-school reactions to a sad scenario were disheartening, to say the least. I share this event and the following reactions to show that we have a culture and society that are not always prepared to identify abuse, and when abuse is found, we may change the subject or dismiss it. Once again, we find a scenario in which men are expected to shut up, man up, get over it, and move on. Men and women may experience abuse, and all those who do should get the needed care and support when such a trauma occurs. Boys should feel neither shame nor judgment in sharing their feelings, vulnerability, and experiences with others.

THE FAMILY JOURNEY

Preventing Road Bumps

Be aware that abuse can happen anywhere, to anyone; teach your son awareness and warning signs. Youth organizations are increasingly aware of the need to implement standards and education to prevent abuse. As one example, USA Swimming, the parent body to many youth club swim programs throughout the country, has an abuse prevention program known as Safe Sport. Safe Sport includes policies, screening, training, monitoring, and mandatory reporting to prevent or recognize abuse cases. Ask your son's extracurricular teams whether they have similar measures in place.

Boys can assault girls. Know, too, that girls can assault boys. Discuss both scenarios with your son. Boys, and girls, are full humans, who deserve the right to withhold consent, and we should believe all children and teens when they come forward about assault.

Substances impair our judgment and reduce our inhibitions, whether we are talking about alcohol or other drugs. The conversations dads and moms have with tween sons about the concept of consent should include the effect that substances may have on impulse control and behaviors. Alcohol limits inhibitions, and it is not permission to pursue what we want without thinking. Similarly, if a peer is under the influence, they are not of sound mind and cannot give consent. Think it's too soon to have these talks with your tween? It's not. Media and peer influences abound, and we parents have more influence with our tweens than we think. A conversation *before* scenarios with alcohol or other drugs arise empowers our sons to make better decisions when the moment does occur. Worried about how to broach such a subject with your tween son? Use examples you come across together in media, and ask open-ended questions when these subjects arise. Ask your son "What do you think?" or even "What do you think you would do in that situation?" to keep the conversation nonjudgmental yet informative for your son. These discussions should occur early and often.

TEACHABLE MOMENTS

Consume Media Together

At the 2022 Academy Awards, Chris Rock made a joke about Jada Pinkett Smith's medical condition, followed by Will Smith walking onstage and slapping Rock in the face. Almost 17 million viewers watched these events unfold, and even if you were not interested in the Oscars, the situation was discussed all over social media, television, classrooms, and workplaces. The scenario is a perfect example of a teachable moment to discuss with your tween and teen sons. An open-ended question of "What are your thoughts on what happened?" is a good conversation starter. This situation has plenty to unpack, as this scenario is not straightforward; both parties engaged in inappropriate behavior. Is it OK to make a joke in a public setting about a medical condition? If someone upsets you, is it OK to react by striking them? How else could this have been handled?

And significantly, the slap occurred to "defend" Jada Pinkett Smith. Does she need to be "defended" by a man? How could she have addressed the inappropriate joke herself (at the time, or later in a different forum)? These are important conversations to have with your son. He will have these conversations anyway; make sure you're a part of them.

In addition, seek out examples of male allyship in the public sphere and point them out to your son. In 2014, Andy Murray, accomplished professional tennis player and Olympic champion, hired a woman, Amelie Mauresmo, as his coach, and a curious phenomenon resulted: if he lost matches, somehow critics derided *her*. Murray noticed this hadn't happened with his previous male coaches and became more outspoken on the issue, writing in 2015 "Have I become a feminist?... Well, if being a feminist is about fighting so that a woman is treated like a man then yes, I suppose I have."[8] Seek out these real-world examples to enrich your family discussions and bring light to important gender-equity issues. I bet your son would be incredulous to learn what is still happening in this day and age.

THE FAMILY JOURNEY

Potholes Along the Route

Internet safety is a moving target for parents. Middle school parents should be aware that online video gaming communities can be influenced by individuals and communities looking to spread subversive messages, misogyny, and even recruit more people to their causes.

In 2016, major league baseball player Chris Sale, not wanting to wear a throwback jersey, cut up all the throwback White Sox uniforms, not just his but the entire team's. Subsequently, some sports media declared it "hilarious," and a commenter stated that that sort of "energy and fire" is part of what makes Sale a "great competitor." When people glorify

---

8. Kay S. Andy Murray's unabashed feminism might be his most admirable legacy. *Sports Illustrated.* January 12, 2019. Accessed May 17, 2023. https://www.si.com/tennis/2019/01/12/andy-murray-retirement-feminism-gender-equality.

emotional dysregulation and society's enabling of toxic behavior, saying "That's just how men are," we're not doing anyone any favors. Not men, not women. Point out these scenarios, ask your son how *his* team would handle such an event if it occurred, and have a conversation about it.

As discussed in Chapters 4, Nurturing Toddlers and Preschoolers to Be Better Men, and 5, Nurturing School-aged Boys to Be Better Men, Common Sense Media is a fantastic resource to help guide family media decisions and to analyze television shows, movies, and video games with a gender equity lens.

Common Sense Media Guidelines

What kids this age learn about gender

- As they experience physical changes of puberty, these create appearance concerns and self-consciousness.
- They feel a greater need to conform to cultural gender norms coinciding with puberty.
- They have concerns about dating.

Common Sense Media goals for media content

- Show messages that worth and happiness do not come from appearance or from physical strength.
- Show role models who participate in dating and relationships in addition to, not instead of, hobbies and other activities.
- Show examples of positive and supportive cross-gender friendships and relationships.
- Show role models who display both feminine and masculine mannerisms, behavior, and career/academic interests without ridicule from other characters.
- Show examples of fully realized transgender characters who experience both ups and downs and are accepted and supported by their peers and communities.

Adapted from Ward LM, Aubrey JS. *Watching Gender: How Stereotypes in Movies and on TV Impact Kids' Development.* Common Sense Media; 2017.

> ## Recommended Film to Discuss With Your Middle School Son
>
> *On the Basis of Sex* [RBG biopic]. Alibaba Pictures; 2018.

WORDS MATTER: PHRASES AT STAGES THAT DO US NO FAVORS

Boys who support women become future male allies. Remind your son that over half the world's population is women. Women's rights *are* human rights. Let's use language to reflect that.

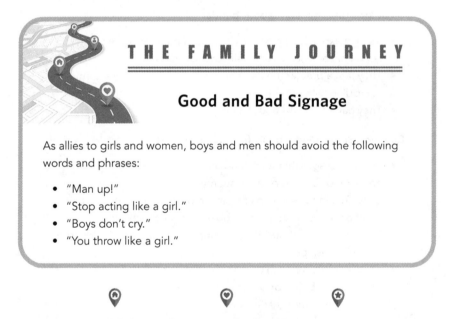

THE FAMILY JOURNEY

Good and Bad Signage

As allies to girls and women, boys and men should avoid the following words and phrases:

- "Man up!"
- "Stop acting like a girl."
- "Boys don't cry."
- "You throw like a girl."

Before you know it, your son will need a checkup with his pediatrician for his high school entry physical examination. Time is supposed to progress along at a steady rate, one second at a time. Experience tells me otherwise. Any parent who has raised a child through high school understands that there must be some form of High School Theory of (Time) Relativity: once your son begins high school, time goes into overdrive. Don't blink, enjoy the fleeting moments, and use the opportunity to nurture values and perspectives that your son can take into his young adulthood to make the world a better, more equitable place.

RECOMMENDED RESOURCES FOR PARENTS OF MIDDLE SCHOOL SONS

Natterson C. *Decoding Boys: New Science Behind the Subtle Art of Raising Sons.* Ballantine Books; 2020.

Reichert MC. *How to Raise a Boy: The Power of Connection to Build Good Men.* TarcherPerigee; 2019.

Chapter 7

Nurturing High School Boys to Be Better Men: Allyship, What Masculinity Can Mean, and Evolving Relationships

On a freezing cold January morning back in 2019, I witnessed an interaction between my high school sons that warmed my heart more than the usual coffee ever could. My oldest was a junior, and for whatever reason that day, my freshman twin sons had to get to school ahead of him. Thanks to the magic of social media "memories" features, I was reminded of this random yet meaningful weekday morning. I have mixed feelings about social media, but I have to admit, it's got me when it reminds me of fun memories from years past.

> "Posting because we always need more positivity in our newsfeeds. 2 of my sons left earlier this morning before their brother. A made M a fruit smoothie and laid out helpful post-it like a treasure hunt to help him find it through his morning haze.

Let's all take care of each other. Also, teenagers are awesome. I'm so
fatigued of the all-too-common refrain that teens are self-centered
and lazy. No one is perfect, we all have bad days, but there's a certain
self-fulfilling prophecy that goes on with the typical lamenting re: teens
from grownups. Let's all demonstrate affection and empathy because kids
do what they see.

And clearly, this house demonstrates love through food!"

The point I was making with this post was that teenagers in general, and teen *boys* specifically, can be caring, loving, self-disciplined, responsible individuals. Is this the messaging that adults typically send teens? Don't fall prey to generations past telling us that teens are self-absorbed. I personally love teenagers because they view the world completely differently than we adults. I've witnessed this not only as a mom but also as a pediatrician with all the intelligent, hilarious, fabulous teenagers I care for in my pediatrics practice. By the time your son is a teen, I hope you've already shared countless conversations and experiences that have shaped his ability to communicate, share feelings, demonstrate empathy, and care for others. Don't blink, because the high school years rev up into overdrive and seem to pass in the blink of an eye. Your son lives under the same roof for just a bit longer; continue to set a high bar of expectations, for expectations become reality. High school is a brief, yet hugely impactful time. Continue the critical conversations needed for your son to broaden his worldview and realize his potential as a full human. Kids live up to our expectations, wherever we set them. Let's set the bar high.

Our teenaged boys are the future men of society. The years of a boy's adolescence are a foundation on which men's views on gender roles, gender expectations, and how people interact with each other at both home and work are solidified. Yes, we also evolve and learn throughout our adult lives, but the teen years are a significantly malleable, impactful time in a boy's life. It is often stated that the human brain continues to develop and mature up through the 25th birthday, so parents would be wise to remember their influence on their sons in this critical, fleeting time span before their sons fly from the family nest toward young adulthood. In this chapter, we will examine how to nurture gender equity in our high school sons, from daily interactions and media consumption, to big-picture views, to a look toward their future as they evolve from classmates to partners in the home and peers in the workplace.

DAILY INTERACTIONS PROVIDE COMMUNICATION OPPORTUNITIES, EMPATHY, EMOTIONAL CONNECTION

In coaching our sons, the skill of empathy is a big-picture parenting goal that is achieved through baby steps taken daily throughout their formative years. Think of empathy as a muscle: with frequent training, use, and stretching, we can nurture this characteristic, not only in our sons but in ourselves. Any good trainer will tell you that stretching 10 minutes once per day is better than stretching 70 minutes once per week. Similarly, nurturing empathy in our kids is a task better accomplished in small, more frequent baby steps.

Modeling empathy to others is the most important because kids do as they see. Make sure *you* do the things, and exhibit the characteristics, you want to see in your teenager. When a loved one asks you a question, put your screen to the side and make eye contact when you answer. Your teenaged son had a bad day? Sit and listen to him, and simply *be* with him, resisting the temptation to interrupt, make suggestions, or problem-solve. Our teens need us parents to be sounding boards, not constant advice givers; with time, they will often arrive at a great solution or resolution of sorts on their own and will appreciate that we showed nonjudgmental support. Your being a good sounding board means your teens will continue to come to you with problems, concerns, and worries, as well as triumphs and funny situations, as time goes on.

When chatting with your teenagers, whether it's a mundane "What should we make for dinner?" conversation or a more heady "My best friend isn't talking to me right now," make sure you *listen* at least as much as you *talk*. After years of being problem-solvers who anticipate situations and swoop in with guidance (or even take over the task, but hopefully you've read previous chapters and know that a takeover doesn't do kids of most ages any favors), parents of teens are wise to step back and let our teens take the wheel, both literally and metaphorically. It is said that by the age of 12 years, our kids already know our opinion and position on pretty much everything, so the teenage years are the age at which we need to talk less and listen more.

We also need to have lots of conversations with our sons about understanding not only girls and women in specific but people in general, especially people living different experiences from our own: people

THE FAMILY JOURNEY

Reading the Signs

When was the last time you said "I trust your judgment" to your teenaged son? This is a powerful statement that I suggest you add to your parenting toolbox. All too often, teenagers do not feel respected by the adults around them, which shuts them down emotionally and reinforces their desire to share the "deep stuff" with only their peers, instead of a parent. "I trust your judgment" is so simple to say, yet it sends a strong message that you trust your teen's instincts to make good choices and come to appropriate conclusions about situations on their own, with your support. When you talk with your teen, listen more and talk less. Know that your son's high school years are the on-deck circle of a baseball metaphor for life. It's best for teens to gain more life experience while still living under your roof than to learn on the fly once they're no longer within the safe haven of home.

across genders, races, and cultural and ethnic backgrounds. For such a high-stakes topic, this task may seem daunting, as if we parents need to perch at a lectern for 2 hours teaching men empathy, to be aware of and curious about others' human experiences. This is *not* the case. In fact, please do *not* perch at a lectern for 2 hours! No one (teenager *or* adult) wants to experience that. Short, digestible nuggets are best. I like to refer to these mini conversations as "stolen moments." Whether the setting is driving in the car, playing catch, or putting away groceries, often the best conversations with our teenagers happen *while we are doing other things.* And when it comes to understanding others, *normalizing* situations and realities can go a long way.

Normalizing others isn't just talk. Friends of mine who are of European white ancestry living in a predominantly white community have made a point to bring their 3 children exclusively to professionals who are people of color. From birth, it was important that their kids understood that people of color are physicians, dentists, and other critical professionals, with bonus points for women of color. They're "walking the walk" to make sure their kids have relationships with people across races in all aspects of their lives, even if it means driving further to appointments to achieve these goals.

As another example of normalizing other people's experiences, our sons may not have personal experience with menstrual issues and all that is involved in the monthly menstrual cycle. Sure, if sisters or moms or family members who have periods live under the same roof, perhaps boys have some exposure, but depending on the family dynamic, that significant portion of girl's, women's, and people's lives may be a complete mystery to your son.

A friend recently shared the following anecdote to her social media:

"I had a conversation with my (high school freshman) son about hysterectomies and menstrual cycles. I told him to never make fun of a girl for accidentally bleeding through her clothes, and that periods are especially difficult for athletes. I also told him girls can have bad cramps.

My son: 'I guess it's like getting kicked in the balls.'

Me: 'Yes. For 3-7 days straight per month.'"

A commenter noted, "I had a similar convo with [my son], and now it's, 'I know, mom. If I see that happened to a girl, I just casually give her my hoodie and tell her if she wants, tie it around her waist, that that's cool.' After said dissertation, he melts into a puddle of embarrassment in front of me, I high-five myself, and everybody lives."

A male commenter added, "Well done. My mother handled that by handing me a book meant to teach girls about what to expect about periods, which had the effect of helping me respect all the [stuff] one has to deal with about menstruation."

I love the above conversation, and the ensuing comments, for many reasons. The matter-of-fact discussion, the teachable moment, and, most of all, the *normalizing* of other people's realities, will widen our sons' worldview to have empathy and greater understanding. Menstrual periods are just one example of many in which we can teach our sons about other genders, cultures, identities, and life experiences.

EMOTIONAL LITERACY AND CONNECTIONS

Create space for your son to form meaningful emotional connections with other boys, whether peers, classmates, teammates, or cross-generational relatives. All too often, boys hold in their emotions and save those deeper conversations for the girls and women in their lives, perpetuating the unfortunate generational trend of women being responsible for "emotional labor" as well as being responsible for "emotional gatekeeping." It's not just women who are good listeners and empathizers; men can serve in these roles as well. Peggy Orenstein, in conversations with adolescent boys and young men, noted a trend of the men confiding mostly to girlfriends, mothers, and sisters. She writes:

> While it's wonderful to know they have *someone* to talk to—and I'm sure mothers, in particular, savor the role—teaching boys that women are responsible for emotional labor, for processing men's emotional lives in ways that would be emasculating for them to do themselves, comes at a price for both sexes. Among other things, that dependence can leave men unable to identify or express their own emotions, and ill-equipped to form caring, lasting adult relationships.[1]

If your son doesn't have boys in his current peer groups who seem to be able to listen and empathize, or worse, who ridicule and make a joke of most situations, that is an issue for parents to explore with their teen son. With your son, consider the following questions:

- Are his current relationships a healthy space?

- Is there reciprocity in the exchange of ideas and feelings?

- Does your son feel emotionally supported by his friendships? If not, what are some strategies your son can use to perhaps meet new people or to strengthen an existing relationship that is currently more of a casual acquaintance?

---

1. Orenstein P. The miseducation of the American boy. *Atlantic*. January/February 2020. Accessed May 18, 2023. https://www.theatlantic.com/magazine/archive/2020/01/the-miseducation-of-the-american-boy/603046.

As with most conversations with teenagers, avoid the temptation to give your son constant suggestions or, worse, to tell your son what to do. Your goal is an open-ended conversation, asking pertinent questions, to help your son think through the issue and arrive at ideas and conclusions on his own.

THE FAMILY JOURNEY

Passengers

Your teen son will hopefully have a variety of friends, including friends of other genders and, likely, friends whose parents have different values from your family's. This is not only OK but healthy. Platonic friendships serve a vital role in supporting our boys' mental health. A variety of values helps your son determine his own views; also, consider that your household may serve as a new perspective for your son's friend.

"Practice" as a teenager means your son will grow into a man who has healthy male friendships. Adult male friendships provide our sons with companionship and safe spaces to share their realities, life's ups and downs, and emotions. Studies have shown that middle-aged men in America have experienced depression at record rates in recent years, with an alarming number of suicide deaths. According to the American Foundation for Suicide Prevention, the rate of suicide is highest among middle-aged white men. In 2020, men died by suicide 3.88 times more than women, with white men accounting for 69.68% of suicide deaths.[2] Let's protect our boys' mental health now and set the stage for our men's mental health for years to come.

Both parents should model adult friendships by being a good friend themselves. All too often, it's easy as a parent to get bogged down in work and family obligations, while our friendships fall by the wayside. Once every few months, we'll text each other "We should get together!" But do we? Friendships, separate from family or romantic partnerships, bolster

---

2. American Foundation for Suicide Prevention. Suicide statistics. Accessed May 18, 2023. https://afsp.org/suicide-statistics.

THE FAMILY JOURNEY

Good Habits for the Road

As a pediatrician, I always have my "developmental stages" hat on. The teen years are significant for peer relationships taking greater importance in your son's life. Male friendships are an aspect of your son's life that will serve him well for years to come. Friendships, even more than romantic partnerships, serve as a buffer and to boost resilience for mental and physical health for decades to come.

As a parent, encourage and support these healthy peer relationships. Better yet, make *your* home a place in which the teens enjoy spending time. Yes, it will increase your grocery bill, but the money is well spent because you'll know who your son's friends are and what sorts of issues they think and talk about. Beyond promoting casual hanging out, I've also hosted pasta parties for my sons' swim teams and cross-country teams (I didn't do all the planning and prep on my own; my sons participated and other team parents pitched in), which were fun ways to meet more of my sons' friends, learn about team dynamics, and have lots of laughs!

our mental health for decades to come, whether we are teens or adults. Let your son witness you as an adult being a good friend.

Life will metaphorically throw us curveballs. Count on it. Divorce, death, illness—these unexpected events and transitions, while challenging, are the opportunities to model and nurture healthy coping strategies, communication, and responses in both sons and daughters. As adults, we can coach our kids through their emotions even as we struggle ourselves. Many families have a generational habit of pushing the adults to be "tough" and to put up a façade of strength in front of younger family members. Kids always know more than the adults around them realize. Teenagers are smart; they know when we are being real, and they will recognize and appreciate our honesty.

As I type this, my family recently dealt with the loss of a great friend (to me) and a second mom figure (to my 4 kids). We are devastated to have lost her: she was a unique, one-of-a-kind individual who not only interacted with my kids daily but supported and nurtured them, and she was going to be a part of our lives for decades to come. She died unexpectedly at too young of an age, and her loss will leave a hole in our hearts. I am grieving and working to support my kids as they process this tragedy. My sons are dealing with the immediate grief in completely distinctive ways, which is to be expected, as they are 3 different people. There is no one correct way to grieve. One of my sons is more forthcoming to talk and tell stories and connect with peers who also knew and loved her. One of my sons has retreated and is playing more video games than usual. I'm working to be present for each of them. I cannot make this better; I cannot fix this. But I can stand alongside my sons. I can support them. I can offer spontaneous hugs. I can check in. I don't have the power to alter the reality, and I can't change this sad situation. But I can listen to my sons, demonstrate empathy, and give them tools they can use as they grow in this life.

HOUSEHOLD CHORES AND THE FAMILY CALENDAR

When our sons were younger, as discussed in earlier chapters, the mental load of family logistics and plans needed to be shared equitably between the adult partners. In middle school, we slowly but surely began to pass the baton to our son himself to coach executive functioning skills and life skills, all the while keeping the adults in the loop. Then, enter high school. High school happens in the blink of an eye, so parents are wise to realize that this is the

Our Family Calendar

Sunday	Monday	Tuesday	Wednesday	Thursday	Friday	Saturday
12	13	14	15	16	17	18
Noon–4:00 pm lifeguarding shift	Track practice after school M—needs the car	Track practice after school Transmission check	Track practice after school Plumber to inspect toilet	Track meet— away meet Dad will pick up boys	Track practice after school	8:00 am noon robotics club

final preparatory stage before "launching" our sons into adulthood. As such, our sons should be the primary driver behind their schedules and logistics.

Carpooling for soccer? Yes, parents can help, but our sons need to start taking the lead on arranging such logistics. In a female-male partnership, if you find that family members are always clarifying logistics with mom daily, it's time to have a family meeting and lay down some new parameters (refer to the "Planning the Route" box in Chapter 6, Nurturing Middle School Boys to Be Better Men).

The default setting for generations has been that moms shoulder the mental load: they know who's picking whom up from school, whether the house is running low on toilet paper, and what dinner will be served. Partners and sons have vital roles to play. If you are a mom, when asked (by an adult or a child) when an event is happening, or what time your son needs to be there, remind your partner or son to look it up themselves. Even if spoon-feeding logistical information was your home's previous default setting, it's not too late to encourage a new way. Have a family meeting and talk about the current state of affairs, and what must change, involving all family members. Learned incompetence (refer to the Family Calendar section in Chapter 6, Nurturing Middle School Boys to Be Better Men) is real, and we moms or partners who have found ourselves in the position of clarifying logistics daily need to make sure we hold our partners and sons accountable. Shared family

THE FAMILY JOURNEY

Planning Family Dinners Together

Life is busy, but there are weekends, summers, and school holidays. When my sons became teenagers, we got into a routine each summer of each boy taking a night of the week to plan and prepare dinner (something more than a bowl of cereal). Examples included simple pasta dishes and from-scratch specialty sandwiches (mmm, Cubanos...). Sure, there were some missteps, some recipes that didn't turn out, and an overcooked item here and there, but this is how we learn and how progress is made. And the next time a coworker mentions that their teen son baked brownies, resist the temptation to respond with shocked incredulity.

calendar apps or a large paper family calendar in the kitchen or another high-traffic area can keep everyone on the same page. If someone drops the ball at some point because of a lack of reminders, in the grand scheme of things, the planet will continue to rotate, and I have a feeling the lesson will be learned for the next time. There can be beauty to the mishaps. Reframe such situations as learning opportunities.

Chores continue to be an important aspect of your son's growth, not only to contribute to the busy household but to develop important life skills. If your son is swamped with too many extracurriculars, consider the big picture. Many of our teenagers are overscheduled, and baseball practice

THE FAMILY JOURNEY

Maintenance

Household chores are as important as ever during your son's teen years. Caring for shared spaces within the home nurture the concept of shared teamwork that will last into adulthood. Personally, I didn't fret about the state of each high school son's bedroom; I simply closed the door, but I expected my sons to manage their own laundry and help clean and care for shared spaces, as well as mow the lawn in the summer and clear the driveway of snow in the winter. Your son's chores should include everything we've discussed in previous, younger-themed chapters plus

- Vacuuming shared spaces (eg, living room, hallways, stairs, furniture)
- Washing and vacuuming the car (*especially* if he has car privileges)
- Mowing the yard, spreading mulch
- Weeding
- Clearing walkways and the driveway of winter snow
- Doing grocery shopping (when he has his driver's license)
- Cleaning the kitchen after meal prep
- Doing pet care (eg, feeding, grooming)
- Helping with/caring for younger siblings

Remember, if your teen son can operate a smartphone, he can figure out how to use a washing machine, an oven, and a dishwasher and can perform many of the needed home tasks.

doesn't make anyone "too busy" to take out the garbage without reminders from a parent. After the age of 16 years, many teens take on part-time work, which is fantastic, but it's not a reason to stop contributing to home chores. Can you imagine if as parents we didn't keep up with household jobs because we "had to go to work"? Make sure your son knows that the work *within* the home is as valuable as the work *outside* the home.

SCHOOL COMMUNICATION

School calendars are often posted online by the start of each academic year, often the preceding spring. High schoolers should take the initiative to make sure they have this calendar at their fingertips. No longer should moms inform sons of events; conversely, *sons* should let dads and moms know what's happening. Days off for college visits? There are lots of logistics involved in arranging college visits, including, but not limited to, communicating the needed days off with the school. All are your son's responsibility to figure out and plan. Trade school open houses? Let your son take the lead on those logistics. These are the cumulative steps necessary to promote our future men's life skills and intentional competence.

TEMPERAMENT, PERSONALITY, EMOTIONAL INTELLIGENCE

For many parents, the suggestions and ideas in this chapter may not exactly be rocket science. After all, each of us is unique and whole, capable of a range of behaviors and emotions. Boys and girls have a variety of temperaments and personalities, and if we examine a random sampling of 100 teenaged boys, of course we will find a significant portion of boys whose empathic, nurturing traits are front and center. This is to be applauded, celebrated, and encouraged. But how often does society, even well-meaning family members, squash certain characteristics in our men? If a teen boy has a rough day, is it acceptable for him to cry? To express himself? Is he given a safe space to say anything about it at all? Our home should be our peaceful haven in which to regroup and recharge for the next day. Home is an environment in which your child should be allowed to be who they are.

At the time of this writing, a viral social media video of a teen boy experimenting with makeup and subsequently discovered by his father was making the rounds. The dad told his son "Whatever you want to do, you'll be OK. I'll be OK with you. I'm with you. I love you." What a different world we would have if we were accepted as our true, full selves, recognized as the unique and whole people we are. Avoid labels. We shouldn't try to fit our kids into a preconceived mold. That will erode a son's self-confidence, and it simply doesn't work. You cannot smush a square peg into a round hole. Meet your son where he is, accept him for the traits and characteristics that make him who he is as an individual, and allow him space to explore, evolve, and navigate his teenage years, with your full support and love.

THE FAMILY JOURNEY

Diverse Routes

Pediatricians love the expression "meet your child where they are." Recognize your teen son for who he is now, including his interests and his passions. It's OK if his journey looks different from your journey or expectations; what a great opportunity for both of you to learn alongside each other, using a growth mindset.

Over the years, we've learned the value of emotional intelligence in our lives. A high IQ is great, but a high EQ, emotional quotient, is just as important because it helps all of us read situations, communicate more effectively, and better understand ourselves and how we affect others. Marc Brackett, PhD, details his RULER system in his book, *Permission to Feel,* used by prekindergarten schools through high schools across the country. RULER stands for *R*ecognizing emotion, *U*nderstanding emotion, *L*abeling emotion, *E*xpressing emotion, and *R*egulating emotion. These concepts make great common sense, and the acronym puts the potentially nebulous world of navigating emotion into context and actionable steps.

In simpler terms, families can use the Golden Rule: Treat others the way you wish to be treated. I've worked to emphasize the Golden Rule as a theme in my house since my now college and high school kids were toddlers. Full disclosure, the more kids you have, the easier it is to enforce the rule because lots of scenarios arise with which to apply the rule. When my kids were toddler and preschool ages, the rule would come up regarding equitable time to play with a particular toy. Now that my kids are older, the rule applies to who gets access to a car on a particular night. Troubleshooting, taking turns, arriving at compromises that have some good for both parties—these are valuable life skills. Negotiating equity in these seemingly minor situations sets the stage for compromise in future relationships with friends, roommates, romantic partners, and coworkers.

TOXIC MASCULINITY VERSUS ASPIRATIONAL MASCULINITY

Dictionary.com defines *toxic masculinity* as "a cultural concept of manliness that glorifies stoicism, strength, virility, and dominance, and that is socially maladaptive or harmful to mental health: *Men and women both suffer when toxic masculinity perpetuates expectations that are restrictive and traumatizing.*"[3] I love that the example sentence used, which puts the phrase into context, points out the ramifications of the cultural concept. Nobody wins with toxic masculinity. Men are pigeonholed into preconceived, restrictive expectations, and women are victimized.

The Me Too movement (and the associated hashtag, #MeToo) became a part of widespread public consciousness in 2017; however, it was born years earlier in 2006 when Tarana Burke coined the phrase on social media. The movement aspires to give voice to people who have survived sexual harassment or outright abuse, and on a broader scope, it seeks to spread empathy. That includes empathy within ourselves to better identify our feelings and regulate our own emotions, as well as empathy toward others for recognizing and responding to their emotions.[4] Me Too spread globally and identified abusive men in power in more than 80 countries.

What are the statistics? Of women, 1 in 4 has experienced rape or attempted rape during their lifetime, according to several national US surveys. Of people surveyed, 81% of women and 43% of men reported experiencing some form of sexual harassment and/or assault in their lifetime, with more than 3 in 4 women (77%) and 1 in 3 men (34%) experiencing verbal sexual

---

3. Dictionary.com. Toxic masculinity. Accessed May 18, 2023. https://www.dictionary.com/browse/toxic-masculinity.
4. Datla A. *Leading With Empathy: Tarana Burke and the Making of the Me Too Movement.* Harvard Kennedy School; 2020.

harassment. More than 47% of those who experienced rape had a perpetrator who was a current or former intimate partner.[5] Clearly, we need to do better.

Empathy is key here. How does a teenaged boy react when his ego is challenged or questioned? Many men respond disproportionately to rejection and, in response, simply "grab" what they want. Pay attention to how your teen son reacts when things don't go well. Be cautious if he takes an "I'll show them" mentality. Grit is wonderful, but when it comes to relationships, being able to let go of those for whom the relationship has weakened is important. Being able to direct one's energies elsewhere in a productive manner is important.

THE FAMILY JOURNEY

Roadblocks

Consent conversations are difficult for parents. Use real-world scenarios and situations in television shows, film, and video games to talk about these important issues. Ask open-ended questions and adopt a tone of curiosity to prevent a judgmental tone.

Does your teen son view a "No" as an initial step, a first offer in an imagined bargaining scenario? Is he listening to the reality in front of him? This question applies to everyday scenarios, not just dating but all relationships. As an example, if you're all on a family outing and he takes pictures of a sibling asleep in the car, step 1, did he have consent to photograph the sleeping sibling? Of course not, because they're asleep! One cannot give consent if they're asleep. Say the sibling is understandably upset at their picture being taken without their consent and watch for how your teenager responds. Does your teen apologize and delete the photo, or does he up the ante by threatening to post the photo to social media? These nonsexual exchanges matter: they are opportunities to remind our teens of boundaries, respect, empathy, and the concept of consent. Being able to accept someone's no is important for relationships of all types throughout

---

5. Me Too. Statistics. Accessed May 18, 2023. https://metoomvmt.org/learn-more/statistics.

our lives. The concept of *consent* continues to be of vital importance in many realms in our daily lives. If consent is a theme reinforced in your home, it will apply to romantic and sexual relationships as well. For more on our teenagers and burgeoning romantic relationships, keep reading.

Sadly, there will be events in the news that remind us that toxic masculinity is alive and well. Although unfortunate, these real-world events should be used by parents as teachable moments. In 2016, Brock Turner received an extremely light 6-month sentence for sexually assaulting an unconscious woman behind a Stanford University campus trash bin. Sadly, you don't need to look too hard for such real-world events. Our teenaged sons need to have discussions with the loving adults in their world, including dads and moms, about why these situations are unjust and wrong. We need to discuss and put these situations into greater context.

Don McPherson, former professional football player, author, and feminist, has noted that gender conversations can lead boys to feel shame and silence. Much of the emphasis is placed on what boys *shouldn't* do rather than who boys *can* be. In an effort to reduce shame in gender conversations, McPherson began using the phrase "aspirational masculinity" in 2019:

> Aspirational masculinity is a way to engage with men in "a positive and deliberate examination of male identity and the relationships and behaviors of and between men.... It is focused on fostering a broader understanding of being male that includes empathy, vulnerability, and emotional honesty around critical issues impacting relationships, sexual behavior, and personal growth."[6]

As a mom of 3 sons, I love this. Discussions about consent are critical; also critical is discussing the breadth of possibilities of what our boys *can* do.

INTERACTIONS WITH EXTENDED FAMILY OR THE GREATER COMMUNITY

Chimamanda Ngozi Adichie's 2012 essay *We Should All Be Feminists*, based on her popular TEDx talk that same year, explores the idea of gender in how we raise our sons and daughters. Adichie states:

---

6. Strauss E. Talking to boys about being a boy. CNN Health. June 10, 2022. Accessed May 18, 2023. https://www.cnn.com/2022/06/10/health/masculinity-conversation-boys-wellness/index.html.

We do a great disservice to boys in how we raise them. We stifle the humanity of boys. We define masculinity in a *very* narrow way. Masculinity is a hard, small cage, and we put boys inside this cage.

We teach boys to be afraid of fear, of weakness, of vulnerability. We teach them to mask their true selves, because they have to be, in Nigerian-speak, a *hard man.*

In secondary school, a boy and a girl go out, both of them teenagers with meager pocket money. Yet the boy is expected to pay the bills, always, to prove his masculinity....

What if both boys and girls were raised *not* to link masculinity and money? What if their attitude was not "the boy has to pay," but rather, "whoever has more should pay"? Of course, because of their historical advantage, it is mostly men who *will* have more today. But if we start raising children differently, then in fifty years, in a hundred years, boys will no longer have the pressure of proving their masculinity by material means.[7]

Personally, I believe that teenagers on a date should simply split the bill, or pay their own way; back as an awkward teenager myself starting to date in 1990 (please don't do the math), I would always insist on splitting the bill. I didn't realize that wasn't commonplace back then. Dating in the 2020s absolutely looks a lot different than the '90s did. The COVID-19 pandemic and resultant waves of variant viruses and subsequent lockdowns have modified social interactions for the bulk of many teens' formative years. Screen time and social media, already in high use, went into overdrive when schools went remote, and teenagers were instructed to shelter in place.

Separate from the pandemic, there was also a shift from one-on-one dates to group dates with friends. This is noticeable not only in high school formal events but also in just routine socializing. Is this a good thing? Perhaps. Gen Z has turned so many "traditional" rites of passage on their heads. To attend my 1992 high school senior prom, a date was required. This is no longer the case, and friends happily group up to attend such events. Ensuring continued conversations with your teens is key. I would just point out that there is not necessarily safety in numbers, so to speak. Parents may have a false sense of security if romantic partnerships are always conducted in group settings, but remember the prevalence of screens. Sexting, including sharing compromising photos, is more commonplace than ever.

---

7. Adichie CN. *We Should All Be Feminists.* Vintage Books; 2012.

A lot of the sexting "warning" conversations facilitated by parents tend to focus on telling our teen girls not to send compromising photos; however, I must point this out: Are we talking with our sons about sexting as well? Have you asked your son what he would do if he were the recipient of such a photo? Or whether he's ever asked for one or even shared one himself? Or whether he's felt pressure to share one? Sexting is a two-way street, and our daughters *and* sons need to consider all the ramifications of this activity, including the potential consequences. Please talk with your son about sexting.

THE FAMILY JOURNEY

Balanced Paths

All too often, topics such as internet or texting safety are directed at girls and women. We tell our daughters don't dress a certain way, don't text certain things, don't be suggestive… Are we having similar conversations with our sons? Are we asking our boys just as many questions? As half the general population, boys and men have a responsibility toward civil, appropriate relationships with others, whether in real life or online.

Similarly, consider conversations about the prevention of sexually transmitted infections and teenage pregnancy. All too often, these conversations are considered as a mandatory lesson for our daughters yet treated as an afterthought for our sons. We must not shy away from discussing these topics with *all* our teens, boys and girls alike. Use resources, and if you're stumped, ask your son's pediatrician at yearly health supervision examinations for advice. Be aware that there is a lot of misinformation not only among peers but on the internet, so it's important for parents to share a voice in educating teenaged boys about sex, choices, and potential outcomes. As just one example, in my clinical practice I've diagnosed chlamydia in plenty of male adolescents, and the typical response to the news is shock and a poor understanding of how the infection was transmitted and what the next steps should be. Our teens need access to quality information, and they deserve conversations with the caring adults in their world.

Consent: we cannot discuss consent enough. Boys should be reminded repeatedly that they must ask for consent when crossing a girl's boundary. A onetime yes is not enough for physical intimacy; it must be an enthusiastic yes. Boys need to know that girls can change their mind; a yes can become a no, and if this occurs, her wishes must be honored. Consent can be withdrawn at any point, at any time.

These are difficult conversations to have with your son. There may be giggling, or your son may shut down emotionally. As unexpected as it seems, it may be best to have this conversation while doing something else. The intensity of a sit-down, make face-to-face eye contact talk might be too much (for either of you). While you drive him home from sports practice, while he helps you put away laundry, while you play catch together... These difficult conversations are often eased if they occur while other things are happening.

Also, keep in mind that the consent conversation is not a "one and done" conversation. Adolescent experts agree that a series of mini conversations on these heady topics is far superior to one big talk. Hearing from dad (or one parent), as well as hearing from mom (or the other parent), provides perspective. When you talk about situations with friends and school peers, or when you watch situations play out in media (even video games), ask open-ended questions, listen, and reinforce the concept of consent. And yes, consent goes both ways; girls should also be aware of the concept for boys.

LOOKING TOWARD THE FUTURE

Making Plans for the Future

High school is a time of planning for the future. Teenagers think about what their interests are, how they enjoy spending their time, and what their goals are, and they start making plans. Interests and talents are not defined by gender. In fact, our organizations and workplaces benefit from a variety of life experiences, perspectives, and opinions. If your goal is to raise a son who promotes gender equity, potential fields of future work should be explored free of a gendered lens. The societal trend has been that the caregiving professions, such as education and nursing, have leaned on female professionals. Just as women can work in male-dominated professions, the opposite should also be true.

Careers With Gender Disparities

Mental health is an example of a field that has been historically dominated by female professionals. In my clinical pediatrics practice, especially with the challenges of the COVID-19 pandemic, I encounter a lot of mental health challenges for children of all ages. The mental health field in general is short-staffed nationally, and we could absolutely use more psychologists, therapists, counselors, licensed clinical social workers, and psychiatrists; too many of our families are on waiting lists, regardless of their insurance. An issue that comes up pretty frequently is, as an example, a 9-year-old boy with family transitions who is struggling in school. How impactful would it be for this boy to have a male counselor? I have plenty of tween and teen male patients who explicitly tell me they prefer a male counselor. Male mental health support professionals are in high demand and will always have their choice of jobs and positions. A male young adult pursing this field is a win-win situation; he'll not only be helping society but also have a robust, booming clinical practice.

StudySoup analyzed data from the National Center for Education Statistics and identified the college majors with the greatest gender disparities. A limitation was that the data were collected through a binary lens, so not all gender identities were represented. Society's biases about who can care for others is reflected in the list that follows. Also, keep in mind that the *college* area of study doesn't reflect *retention:* what percentage of women *stay* in fields for the next 10, 20, and 30 years. As an example, women account for 20% of all engineering graduates, but a significant portion of these women later on work in different fields or quit altogether. Here are the statistics on college areas of study.

- Information technology (software developers, web developers, programmers, and security analysts): 80% male, 20% female, with even smaller numbers for women of color
- Animal sciences (veterinarians): 80% female
- Public health: 81% female
- Computer science: 82% male
- Computer and information sciences (programmers): 82% male

- Electrical and electronic engineering: 80% male
- Mechanical engineering: 86% male
- Human services, social work: 86% female
- Computer engineering: 87% male
- Nursing (registered nurses): 88% male
- Special education and teaching, general: 89% female
- Elementary education and teaching: 92% female
- Human development and family studies (social workers, marriage or family therapists, and rehabilitation counselors): 92% female
- Early childhood education and teaching: 96% female[8]

Let's normalize our male young adults pursuing fields known for caring for others. If your son mentions interest in underrepresented fields, you'll want to be aware of any preconceived notions or biases you may harbor and to keep an open mind. Our young adults' futures are *theirs,* not ours; it's our job to educate our young adults to the many possibilities open to them and to support them on their unique, individual journeys.

THE FAMILY JOURNEY

Diverse Routes

Whether your son goes on to trade school, college, or work straight out of high school, have conversations about all potential career fields. Being male in a female-dominated field not only moves the societal needle toward greater gender equity but also means he'll be in demand because of his unique position.

8. College majors with the greatest gender disparities. *Chicago Tribune.* August 3, 2021. Accessed May 18, 2023. https://www.chicagotribune.com/business/careers-finance/sns-stacker-majors-gender-disparities-20210803-3rhi7s4vgvdhln4tjngcokmh2a-photogallery.html.

A Sign of Support

Male allies can be found in all career disciplines. In a letter to the editor of the school student newspaper, Jared Mauldin, at the time, a senior in mechanical engineering at Eastern Washington University, a historically male-dominated field, wrote:

To the women in my engineering classes:

While it is my intention in every other interaction, I share with you to treat you as my peer, let me deviate from that to say that you and I are in fact unequal.

Sure, we are in the same school program, and you are quite possibly getting the same GPA as I, but does that make us equal?

I did not, for example, grow up in a world that discouraged me from focusing on hard science.

Nor did I live in a society that told me not to get dirty, or said I was bossy for exhibiting leadership skills.

In grade school I never had to fear being rejected by my peers because of my interests.

I was not bombarded by images and slogans telling me that my true worth was in how I look, and that I should abstain from certain activities because I might be thought too masculine.

I was not overlooked by teachers who assumed that the reason I did not understand a tough math or science concept was, after all, because of my gender.

I have had no difficulty whatsoever with a boy's club mentality, and I will not face added scrutiny or remarks of my being the "diversity hire."

When I experience success the assumption of others will be that I earned it.

So, you and I cannot be equal. You have already conquered far more to be in this field than I will ever face.

Reproduced from Pittman T. Male engineering student perfectly explains why female classmates aren't his equals. HuffPost.com. Updated October 9, 2015. Accessed May 18, 2023. https://www.huffpost.com/entry/women-men-engineers-arent-equal-jared-mauldin-letter_n_561699b9e4b0e66ad4c6bee5.

EQUITY ALLIES IN THE CLASSROOM AND THE HOUSEHOLD, FUTURE ALLIES IN THE WORKPLACE

In a May 2021 interview that aired on the NPR Chicago station WBEZ, former President Barack Obama spoke to Aarti Shahani regarding his thoughts about what it means to be a man in current times. Regarding boys' interactions with others, Obama said:

> I think what we haven't spent as much time doing is thinking about "What are the positive values that we're trying to instill, in our boys, so that, when they grow up, they are respectful, thoughtful partners with women, whether it's in the family or the workplace? What are those things that are not constructed based on the man being able to do what he wants and then the woman adjusting, but rather, how do we meet as equals and...work together to raise families, build businesses, make the world a better place?"[9]

This evokes a comic panel a friend recently texted me, in which a man is on bended knee proposing to a woman. He says to her "Would you do me the honor of taking on even more responsibilities while my life remains largely unchanged?"[10] All too often, the default setting is for the woman in a female-male partnership to make adjustments; let's allow young men to make adjustments to support their partners as well.

I have given inequity among partnerships a lot of thought. I really scratch my head in confusion when I think about all the female leaders we have in high schools across the country yet such a low percentage of female CEOs among the Fortune 500 companies, as just one example. The high school environment is a relatively egalitarian place in which women can easily be student council presidents, lead peer-advising groups, and set the curve on STEM exams. What happens later that causes a shift from this seemingly ideal equity? My short answer is that women are the ones who give birth, and with all that that entails, the archaic notion that the woman is the "default parent" persists.

Obama is referencing a very real situation in which a modern female-male partnership can be unbalanced in goal setting and mutual support. In fact, I would argue that the balance is so off that many women don't

9. Shahani A. *Art of Power*. Barack Obama redefines what it means to be a man. May 13, 2021. Accessed May 18, 2023. https://www.wbez.org/stories/barack-obama-redefines-what-it-means-to-be-a-man/9cb514f8-7d89-43da-8912-b34399789771.

10. Cartoons from the September 14, 2020, issue. *The New Yorker*. September 7, 2020:3. Accessed May 18, 2023. https://www.newyorker.com/cartoons/issue-cartoons/cartoons-from-the-september-14-2020-issue.

even voice their goals, or they don't realize that their wishes are even an option. The day-to-day, hectic schedule of raising kids, feeding everyone, and running a household is more than a full-time job, and many women cannot even dream of what they'd like to do, if given the opportunity, in an ideal world. Are you aware of households in which the man navigates the day-to-day to allow the woman to pursue her career goals? I have several medical school friends for whom this is the case. I argue that this is also possible for at least chunks of time, alternating which partner is receiving the bulk of the support. Life occurs in phases; there may be a 4-year stretch in which the male partner advances his career, followed by a 5-year stretch in which the majority of the household support flows toward the female partner to help her achieve *her* particular goals.

THE FAMILY JOURNEY

Don't Be Afraid to Pivot

Parenthood, and life, is ever-changing. Our current routine isn't forever. Parents can take turns focusing on career, pivoting, and then focusing on family and supporting the other parent every 4 years or so. Similarly, let's coach our sons in the flexibility to be the kind of partner who can support and encourage a partner during these transitions, serving as an ally to a partner pursuing specific career goals.

Working moms are setting the stage for more enlightened future male populations simply by existing and normalizing that experience for our sons. If you're a working mom, particularly in a female-male partnership, replace working-mom guilt with a pat on your own back knowing that it's not the female partner's role in the household to micromanage or to ensure that every cog in the wheel runs smoothly. I, personally, have struggled with this because my kids' friends have a range of family situations, and we're human and can't help but compare. Single working parents are wise to delegate more responsibility to their teen children anyway. It's a win-win situation: teens who do laundry, can prepare a simple meal for the family, and can complete necessary school forms on time not only help the household run more smoothly but gain valuable life skills immensely useful in the future. And on those inevitable occasions when things are missed or completely screwed up? In these cases, there can be beauty in the mishaps, which will serve as life lessons for your teens.

In a gender-equitable world, men are *allies* for female empowerment. In the workplace, gender equity benefits all parties and, frankly, results in more profits when businesses account for female perspectives and experiences. Authors David Smith and W. Brad Johnson write about allyship in the workplace in their book *Good Guys*. Smith stated in an interview about the book, "There's a gap between what men say they believe, and what they are actually doing. It's the same as the conversation around race: It's not enough to say you're not a racist, you have to actually do something to create change and take action."[11] It's not enough to believe in equity; men need to advocate for equity through both words and actions.

Let's talk with our sons about the dynamic in their classrooms in high school. Also, let's talk with them about the dynamic at work when they take on part-time jobs later in high school. Have they witnessed gender inequity at school or work? Has a situation arisen in which they felt they needed to speak up for a girl, or further, did they feel they should have spoken up but didn't? Do they ensure their peers have equal talking time in classroom discussions? If a coworker at their job is making derogatory remarks about female coworkers (or anyone who has been marginalized to "other" at all, whether culturally, ethnically, or socioeconomically), are they brave enough to, at a minimum, ask the open-ended question "Why would you say that?" Your conversations about these issues will help plant seeds now that will grow into more equitable workplaces for everyone in the future.

One example of a "female" perspective that effected progress in a male-dominated field is that of Daina Taimiņa, a mathematician. The male-dominated field of mathematics struggled to find ways to explain the geometry concept of hyperbolic planes, but Taimiņa's hobby of crochet allowed her to teach, explain, and demonstrate hyperbolic planes in a far superior fashion to flimsy paper models. Either more men need to crochet or perhaps they can realize how much is to be learned from a perspective different from their own.

Patriarchal ideas surround us, and books are yet another example of where progress is needed. It is estimated that female readers will read

11. Taylor C. Good guys: how men can be allies to women at work. *Reuters*. November 17, 2020. Accessed May 18, 2023. https://www.reuters.com/article/world-work-goodguys-idINL1N2I21VB.

roughly a 50:50 ratio of books written by men and women, and for male readers, the ratio is 80:20. Mary Ann Sieghart writes of this issue that part of it is in how we train boys to read, perhaps because educators

> [A]re worried about boys reading less than girls, [so] the curriculum is massively skewed the other way. Recent research by End Sexism in Schools (a UK based grassroots organization) found [that]…77% of schools teach only one or no whole texts by female writers out of nine, 82% of novels have a male protagonist and 99% of plays are by men. If we don't inculcate the habit of reading widely [when boys are younger], it's going to be harder for men to learn it when they are older.[12]

Read a variety of materials featuring a diverse array of authors, and encourage your son to do the same.

ROLE MODELING AS PARENTS

In the NPR interview mentioned earlier in this chapter, Obama spoke about his experience growing up without a father-figure in the home:

> Partly because I grew up without a father in the home, I had to spend time thinking about, all right, what does it mean to be a full-grown man? There are a lot of ideas of strength, masculinity, power that are defined by dominance and subordination. Sadly, in our society and in our world, it's often defined by violence, or the capacity for violence and force; money; and what money can buy. I think that oftentimes…the narrow definitions that we provide our boys growing up, about what it means to be strong, powerful, admired, a man, seep into how we think about public policy and how we organize our societies and, often, [are] a stunted view and that part of what we have to do is to expand our notions of manhood and power so that providing people health care, caring for children, and being good stewards of the environment, that's what men do, as opposed to just going to war and…making lots of money and, you know, telling other people what to do.[13]

---

12. Sieghart MA. Books by women that every man should read: chosen by Ian McEwan, Salman Rushdie, Richard Curtis and more. *The Guardian*. May 28, 2022. Accessed May 18, 2023. https://www. theguardian.com/books/2022/may/28/books-by-women-that-every-man-should-read-chosen-by-ian-mcewan-salman-rushdie-richard-curtis-and-more.

13. Shahani A. *Art of Power*. Barack Obama redefines what it means to be a man. May 13, 2021. Accessed May 18, 2023. https://www.wbez.org/stories/barack-obama-redefines-what-it-means-to-be-a-man/9cb514f8-7d89-43da-8912-b34399789771.

That's a lot to unpack right there. But on the simplest terms, let's think about how we limit ourselves when we talk about "what men do" and "what women do." Families with single parents and same-gender parents may have an advantage here, as household tasks simply need to get done, no matter what gender the parent is. In contrast, female-male partnerships should put active thought into the division of labor. An effort should be made to include teenagers in household chores as much as possible, as valuable life skills are learned this way (and, let's be honest, it's a lot of work to run a household). Just as dads can grocery shop, cook dinner, wash kitchen floors, and wash and fold laundry, so, too, can teenagers. Additionally, ensure that the assignment of home chores to your teenagers doesn't fall along gender lines. Sons can prepare dinner, and daughters can mow the lawn and take out the garbage. Rotate chores as needed over time, but make the chores equitable. On holidays, birthdays, and major family events, make sure sons help with cooking, serving food, and cleaning up. We need to continue to model equity and not leave these events to the girls and women to plan, execute, and clean up afterward.

THE FAMILY JOURNEY

Viewing the Horizon

Single working parents have the advantage of demonstrating to sons what it means to juggle work, family, and life circumstances. Unpack the guilt and know that your teen son's perspective and experiences will make him a better, more empathic, teamwork-inclined man.

TEACHABLE MOMENTS

Consume Media Together

The way men are portrayed in media is, thank goodness, evolving, and it's been great to have men represented as fully fleshed-out characters, with vulnerable and empathic aspects to their personalities, shine on our screens. *Ted Lasso* is an excellent example of this: The streamed television series that premiered in 2020 centers on an American football coach who is hired to coach an English soccer team. The magic of the ensemble cast shines as we get to know a variety of characters with diverse backgrounds, both in culture and in personality. Sam Obisanya is a 21-year-old footballer (Americans: read "soccer player") from Nigeria and, despite the miles from home, manages to stay in frequent contact with his father via text messaging and phone calls, debunking the societal myth of a young man simply "leaving" his family. He confides in his father, seeks his father's counsel when grappling with decisions, and, casting aside any preconceived notions about the behaviors of young adults who play professional sports, regularly tells his father "I love you, Daddy," who then always reciprocates these expressions of affection back to Sam. I love that the writers of *Ted Lasso* have given us examples of men in touch with their feelings, speaking their feelings, which is all the more powerful in the typically machismo context of professional sports. In fact, one of Lasso's best quotes is "Be curious, not judgmental." What a world this would be if more people, men and women alike, followed that motto.

Media and the internet are rife with examples of toxic masculinity and gender-role assumptions. Watch television shows and movies together, and talk about them. Open-ended questions are best: "What did you think about the way he talked to her?" Again, avoid the metaphorical 2 hours at a lectern. One or two thought-provoking questions are sufficient. Avoid preaching, and encourage a *conversation*.

THE FAMILY JOURNEY

Potential Potholes

Online video gaming is a form of social media. Be aware of, ask questions, and even join in video gaming with your teen son if asked. You may feel foolish (I sure did), but playing video games with your son is great bonding time while learning more about his interests. Families should be aware of influencers and hidden communities that reside within the networks; some groups actively recruit to their causes online. Awareness is prevention.

My then high school sons and I watched Serena Williams play Naomi Osaka in the US Open final live in September 2018. A chain of events occurred in which the (male) chair umpire made a series of calls against Williams, in that we will never fully know who truly deserved to win the match. Osaka's victory was tainted for both women. At the time, Chris Evert said, "I've been in tennis a long time, and I've never seen anything like it." While watching the events unfold in real time in our living room, I couldn't shake the feeling of Serena representing women returning to work after having a baby, and I was talking to the television, saying "Serena, don't cry; Serena don't cry," and 2 of my teen sons said to me "Why can't she cry? It shows she cares. Crying is not a sign of weakness." To hear my sons say this to me was overwhelming. What an important perspective to consider. It was at that point that *I* began to cry myself.

Common Sense Media Gender-Equity Guidelines

What teens this age learn about gender

- Their gender stereotyping becomes more flexible.
- Their ideas about careers, occupational roles, and work become salient; these ideas can be based in gender stereotypes.
- They feel an increased need to learn gender-based expectations for how to behave in romantic and sexual situations.
- Their appearance concerns continue.

Goals for media content

- Show portrayals that show boys and men expressing their emotions constructively, having diverse interests (not only interests in sex), and being accepting of gay characters.
- Show portrayals that steer away from gender-based racial stereotypes.
- Show teens who have non-gender–stereotypical professional aspirations (eg, girls who want to be scientists, boys who want to be nurses) and adult characters who are successful and fulfilled in both traditional and nontraditional professions.
- Show diverse dating scripts that are not steeped in gender stereotypes (eg, boys who always make the first move, girls who are passive and acquiescent).

(continued on next page)

- Show sexual scenarios in which gender is not the driving force behind how sexual partners behave and in which both partners have agency.
- Show female characters who set sexual boundaries and who are comfortable with voicing their needs.
- Show cross-gender relationships that are based on nonromantic or nonsexual friendship and trust.

Adapted from Ward LM, Aubrey JS. *Watching Gender: How Stereotypes in Movies and on TV Impact Kids' Development*. Common Sense Media; 2017.

WORDS MATTER: PHRASES AT STAGES THAT DO US NO FAVORS

Between my 3 sons, their friend circles, extracurriculars, and athletic teams, on a family level and on a social level, I have been firmly ensconced in the world of teen boys. Additionally, having worked in my clinical pediatrics practice for years, I have developed quite a bond with the "boy families" for whom I care; these families know full well that I have 3 sons of my own. A particular joy of my job is that we all get to "grow up" together. I've often joked that I speak "fluent boy."

That said, because I'm surrounded by teenaged boys at both home and work, I'm a frequent observer of the language we use surrounding our young boys as they're growing. Probably the first thought that comes to mind is if, as an example, as a mom, I mention that my son cooked dinner for us last night (in a conversation either in real life or on social media), most of the responses are somewhat incredulous, even bitter. "I wish my son did that" or "How did you convince him to do that?" are frequent responses. Why are these events or behaviors considered such odd events, such outliers? These events don't magically begin overnight; baby steps, daily choices, and small decisions all add up. Rome wasn't built in a day, so normalize boys' participation in cooking in the kitchen, normalize boys' comfort with preparing food, or normalize any other "traditionally female" household task.

When my kids were small, other families warned me that once your child starts high school, time starts to speed up. The Star Wars fan in me agrees that watching your teen's high school years is like sitting in the Millennium Falcon's cockpit as it launches into hyperspace, with stars zooming toward you. Although adolescence is a developmental period defined by the fact that our teens' "outside" world of friends, peers, and school becomes more important than ever, parents and family are still primary influences in a teen's life. We are a teenager's safe landing spot, we are their history, we are their sounding board as they learn more about themselves and their relationships with others, and, significantly, we bear witness as they form their ideas and habits and unearth biases about gender, gender roles, and gender equity. Our teenagers are future adults, and their approach to gender equity will become the new societal and cultural patterns and norms. Be present with your teenager, take advantage of the opportunities that arise to discuss gender roles, and move the needle closer to equity to effect generational change.

SUGGESTED BOOKS AND FILMS FOR HIGH SCHOOL BOYS

- Brackett M. *Permission to Feel: The Power of Emotional Intelligence to Achieve Well-being and Success.* Celadon Books; 2019. Brackett is the founding director of the Yale Center for Emotional Intelligence and the creator of the RULER system, an evidence-based systematic approach to social-emotional learning that has been adopted by more than 2,000 schools, prekindergarten schools through high schools. This is a good read for both boys and parents.
- Kaufman M. *The Time Has Come: Why Men Must Join the Gender Equality Revolution.* Counterpoint; 2019. Kaufman is the cofounder of the White Ribbon Campaign, the international network of men working to end violence

against women, and advises on gender equality to the United Nations, governments, nongovernmental organizations, schools, and workplaces.

- McPherson D. *You Throw Like a Girl: The Blind Spot of Masculinity*. Edge of Sports; 2019. NFL veteran Don McPherson, the feminist activist who coined the phrase "aspirational masculinity," examines how a narrow definition of masculinity adversely affects women and creates ignorance that hinders the healthy development of men.
- Miller C. *Know My Name*. Viking; 2019. A memoir from a sexual assault survivor.
- Shetterly ML. *Hidden Figures: The American Dream and the Untold Story of the Black Women Mathematicians Who Helped Win the Space Race*. William Collins; 2016.
- Smith DG, Johnson WB. *Good Guys: How Men Can Become Better Allies for Women in the Workplace*. Harvard Business School Publishing Co; 2020. Gender-in-the-workplace experts David G. Smith and W. Brad Johnson counter the perception that gender-inclusion initiatives are the responsibility of women. Men are often the most influential coworkers in an organization; male allies help women and men alike.
- *This Changes Everything*. Documentary. CCV Studios; 2018. An investigative analysis of gender inequity in Hollywood, featuring accounts from well-known actors and executives in the industry.

Chapter 8

Young Men Who Promote Gender Equity When They Leave Our Homes: Small Steps Add Up to Generational Changes

How do people make the world a better place? It's a lofty goal, but changing the world begins with each and every one of us. Small steps, daily choices, intentional actions, helping each other... These all make a difference.

After months of rising tensions, in February 2022, Russia launched an invasion of Ukraine. These world events make us question humanity and the course that our civilization is taking. As individuals and as families living on the other side of the planet, we may realize that this conflict is far beyond our personal control. Closer to home, turn on the local news and you'll watch reports of abuse or gun violence. It's easy to feel helpless.

SMALL STEPS

It is exactly in these moments, however, that I try to focus my attention on matters that *are* under our control. We can take daily, actionable steps to influence our sons, our families, and our communities in which we live and work.

At the time of this writing, my daughter, my fourth of 4 kids, was taking trigonometry/precalculus as a high school sophomore. A big test was coming up and she was panicking because she felt that some important concepts weren't covered well during class. I didn't know about any of this situation until a couple days *after* said exam, during a conversation in which she was, with rapid-fire delivery, updating me on the current state of her life and then offhandedly mentioned that she was beside herself, not sure what to do, so she texted her oldest brother, a second-year student studying electrical engineering in college at the time. As she's relaying the situation way after the fact (and well after the exam, in which she performed quite capably), she pulled out her phone to show me a lengthy exchange between her and her brother including examples and illustrations he created on his tablet to help convey the necessary concepts. I understood none of it (I was a premedical history major in college), but despite my ignorance, reading their long text exchange thread brought happy tears to my eyes. My daughter needed support and she knew she could reach out to her (extremely busy) college brother who dropped everything to spend the time to ensure that she not only understood but mastered these concepts. My young adult son recognized the value in connection, the talent he has with which to help others; boosted his own self-esteem; and experienced the joy of paying it forward. Parenthood is a long journey, but to witness this young man demonstrating empathy, providing support, and setting aside his busy schedule to help his loved one, with zero involvement from a parent... Wow. One of the most humbling parenting moments I have experienced.

As a pediatrician, when I examine a newborn baby in my clinic with his proud parents looking on, I not only point out typical newborn physical examination findings but also talk about the young man he will eventually grow to be. I realize it is mind-boggling for new parents to imagine this small, 7-pound wrapped bundle years down the line as a walking, talking, independently thinking young adult. Rome wasn't built in a day, a journey begins with one small step followed by another, and our daily choices and actions influence our future men, and our society, more than we realize. There will be busy weeks when we are focused on logistics and survival and that is OK, but make sure you take the time here and there to pause, step back, consider the big picture, think about your family's goals, and make shifts, where needed, to nurture your boy to be a better man. Gender equity starts at home.

Thank you for engaging in this important conversation with me. The fact that you took the time with this book means that you are intentional and you're already helping move the needle of progress toward improved generational gender equity. Continue these conversations with your son, your partner, your family, your friends, your community, and, most importantly, yourself. Identify the moments when you've stumbled or failed (these setbacks *will* happen despite your best intentions), and use a growth mindset to view these situations as teachable moments. Celebrate the wins, and realize where and how we can do better. We've come so far, and as a fellow parent of boys, I'm hopeful and optimistic that even better is yet to come.

Appendix

More Gender Equity Recommended Reading, Media, and Resources

Also, please note the age-appropriate recommendations at the end of each chapter.

READING

Black MI. *A Better Man: A (Mostly Serious) Letter to My Son.* Algonquin Books of Chapel Hill; 2020

Doyle G. *Untamed.* Dial Press; 2020

Jha S. *How to Raise a Feminist Son: Motherhood, Masculinity, and the Making of a Family.* Sasquatch Books; 2021

Kindlon D, Thompson M. *Raising Cain: Protecting the Emotional Life of Boys.* Ballantine Books; 1999

Kisner J. Boy, uninterrupted. *Atlantic.* October 2019. Accessed May 18, 2023. https://www.theatlantic.com/magazine/archive/2019/10/boy-uninterrupted/596656

Orenstein P. *Boys & Sex: Young Men on Hookups, Love, Porn, Consent, and Navigating the New Masculinity.* Harper; 2020

Parker J. The cartoon that captures the damaged American male. *Atlantic.* October 2018. Accessed May 18, 2023. https://www.theatlantic.com/magazine/archive/2018/10/rick-and-morty-masculinity/568306

Perez CC. *Invisible Women: Data Bias in a World Designed for Men.* Abrams; 2019

Rosin H. *The End of Men: And the Rise of Women.* Riverhead Books; 2012

MEDIA

Hidden Figures. Movie. Fox 2000 Pictures; 2016

On the Basis of Sex [RBG biopic]. Alibaba Pictures; 2018

This Changes Everything. Documentary. CCV Studios; 2018
Looks at gender disparity in Hollywood.

PODCAST

Durante C, Loftus J. *The Bechdel Cast.* Accessed May 18, 2023
About the portrayal of women in movies, hosted by Caitlin Durante and Jamie Loftus.

WEBSITES

American Academy of Pediatrics. Accessed May 18, 2023. https://www.HealthyChildren.org
HealthyChildren.org is the official American Academy of Pediatrics website for parents.

The Good Men Project. Accessed May 18, 2023. https://goodmenproject.com
From the website: "...Our content reflects the multidimensionality of men—we are alternately funny and serious, provocative and thoughtful, earnest and light-hearted. We search far and wide for new stories and new voices from 'the front lines of modern manhood.' And we do it without moralizing and without caricaturizing

our audience; we let guys be guys, but we do it while challenging confining cultural notions of what a 'real man' must be.

Guys today are neither the mindless, sex-obsessed buffoons nor the stoic automatons our culture so often makes them out to be. Our community is smart, compassionate, curious, and open-minded; they strive to be good fathers and husbands, citizens and friends, to lead by example at home and in the workplace, and to understand their role in a changing world."

The Mankind Project USA. Accessed May 18, 2023. https://mkpusa.org

From the website: "The ManKind Project is men's community for the 21st century. MKP is a nonprofit training and education organization with three decades of proven success hosting life-changing experiential personal development programs for men. MKP supports a global network of free peer-facilitated men's groups and supports men in leading lives of integrity, authenticity, and service. …We believe that emotionally mature, powerful, compassionate, and purpose-driven men will help heal some of our society's deepest wounds. We support the powerful brilliance of men and we are willing to look at, and take full responsibility for, the pain we are also capable of creating—and suffering. We care deeply about men, our families, communities, and the planet."

Orenstein P. Positive sexuality. Peggy Orenstein. Accessed May 18, 2023. https://www.peggyorenstein.com/positive-sexuality

Smiler A. Books and videos. Andrew Smiler, Ph.D. Accessed May 18, 2023. https://andrewsmiler.com/books

Dr Smiler is an author and licensed therapist with expertise in adolescent boys, men, and masculinity, who has examined the history of Western masculinity.

Acknowledgments

As an only daughter with older brothers, born to a mom with a brother and no sisters, and a dad with 4 brothers and no sisters, who then went on myself to have 3 boys and 1 daughter, I've lived in a male-dominated family my whole life. I've thought a lot about gender roles within families and within society and I am grateful to add my voice to the continued conversations we still must have to effect generational change. I am grateful for parents who didn't allow gender to play a role in my ambitions and for my brother Todd who has used his public platform within the film industry to serve as a vocal ally for women in his traditionally male-dominated field.

A huge thank-you to the many families with whom I conversed about raising our sons for a more gender-equitable world, especially:

- The Bissell Horvath Family
- The Burke Family
- The Heinz Family
- The Henderson Family
- The Hillegass Family
- Theresa Berdiel-Johnson
- The Kelly Family
- The Magloire Family
- Bonnie Groen Olson, PhD
- Priyanka Patel, MD
- The Wallek Family
- The Williams Family

Thank you to Nerissa Bauer, MD, FAAP, and David Hill, MD, FAAP, for technical review.

A special note of gratitude to Theresa Berdiel-Johnson, certified reading specialist and first-grade teacher, for her research and expertise on quality children's books that both broaden kids' perspectives and promote gender equity.

And to my own 4 children, Matthew, Andrew, Ryan, and Nancy, who are now young adults. Having a front row seat to witness your growth and hear your perspectives on all matters, big and small, has enriched my life in indescribable ways. I love you all and am so grateful for each and every one of you.

Index